Weaving Western Sakiori

A Modern Guide for Rag Weaving

Amanda Robinette

STACKPOLE
BOOKS

Guilford, Connecticut

Published by Stackpole Books
An imprint of The Rowman & Littlefield Publishing Group, Inc.,
4501 Forbes Blvd., Lanham, MD 20706
Distributed by NATIONAL BOOK NETWORK
800-462-6420

Photography by Kathy Eckhaus unless otherwise credited
Illustrations by Caroline Stover unless otherwise credited

We have made every effort to ensure the accuracy and completeness of
these instructions. We cannot, however, be responsible for human error,
typographical mistakes, or variations in individual work.

British Library Cataloguing in Publication Information Available

Library of Congress Cataloging-in-Publication Data

Names: Robinette, Amanda, author.
Title: Weaving western sakiori : a modern guide for rag weaving / Amanda
  Robinette.
Description: Guilford, Connecticut : Stackpole Books, [2018]
Identifiers: LCCN 2018010332 (print) | LCCN 2018014821 (ebook) | ISBN
  9780811767569 (e-book) | ISBN 9780811716093 (paperback : alk. paper)
Subjects: LCSH: Rag rugs. | Hand weaving--Patterns.
Classification: LCC TT850 (ebook) | LCC TT850 .R566 2018 (print) | DDC
  746.7/4--dc23
LC record available at https://lccn.loc.gov/2018010332

⊖™ The paper used in this publication meets the
minimum requirements of American National Standard
for Information Sciences—Permanence of
Paper for Printed Library Materials, ANSI/NISO
Z39.48-1992.

Printed in the United States of America

CONTENTS

Beginning with the Basics: Scarves and Sampling

Basic Western Sakiori Scarf
32

Bright Bamboo Scarf
36

Recycled Silk Strip Yarn Scarf
40

Elongated Twill Scarf
44

Bamboo Overshot Scarf
48

Dogwood Flower Overshot
Scarf with Tencel 52

Making Memories

Mom's Housecoat Mug Rugs
58

Walking on Sunshine
T-shirt Rug 64

Cozy Flannel Baby Blanket
70

Colors of the Caribbean Baby Blanket 74

Wedding Dress Bed Runner 80

For the Home

Under the Sea Desk Runner 88

Sundown Wall Hanging 92

Rustic Wool Hearth Rug and Log Carrier 96

Weaving to Wear

Flower Garden Overshot Shawl 104

I See Fire: Keyhole Scarf with Beads 110

Men's Vintage Bowling Shirt 116

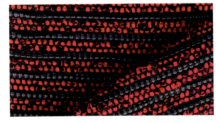

Elegant Evening Bag with Silk and Leather 120

A Necktie for the Modern Gentleman 124

Sodenashi 128

FOREWORD

When I first became interested in sakiori, I was disappointed to discover that there were few sources of information about it, particularly in English. I spent a lot of time on the internet and leafing through long books about Japanese folk crafts to find any mention of it, and I gathered any tidbits I could find.

While this book is not intended to be a history book but rather a weaving book, I have taken the opportunity to present an overview of what I have learned from many sources over the years, so that other weavers would not need to spend quite as much time researching to gain a basic understanding.

The main purpose of this book is to teach you what you need to know about sakiori to start doing it on your own, and in your own way. There is a sett chart for rag weaving with common warp yarns, a wet-finishing chart, instructions for finding and preparing rags, weaving instructions, and some advice for weaving sakiori on rigid heddle looms.

There are also projects with instructions, but it is my intention that you take these projects as ideas and inspiration, not necessarily to duplicate them. This would be a difficult feat, anyway, since every rag is different. Your wedding dress is not likely to be of the same fabric as the one with which I wove the Wedding Dress Bed Runner (p. 80), and you are unlikely to be able to find exactly the same colored skirts I used for the Colors of the Caribbean Baby Blanket (p. 74).

My hope is that, with the general instructions and these projects for inspiration, you will make your own sakiori, and make it into many beautiful and interesting things. I love to see what my students do with their sakiori, and if you would like to share your projects with me as well, please do, and let me know if it is all right for me to share with others on my blog or on social media.

As much fun as I have watching how each idea of mine turns into reality, I am more excited to put my ideas out there and see how other weavers make them their own.

Happy weaving!

Amanda

www.AmandaRobinette.com
Blog: www.westernsakiori.com
Facebook: Western Sakiori
E-mail: westernsakiori@gmail.com

Saku, *Japanese, to tear or rip*
Oru, *Japanese, to weave*
Sakiori, *Japanese, a method of rag weaving used in Japan*
by peasant or rural populations from approximately the mid-18th through the
mid-20th century for the construction of work garments, obis, and other utilitarian textiles

Introduction

Most North American and European weavers at some point in their weaving education choose to try weaving with rags, usually making a rag rug or some place mats. It is part of our cultural tradition, and there are many beautiful examples, particularly in northern European countries such as Sweden and Finland. When we make rag rugs we feel a kinship with the colonists who settled on our continent from those European countries, and a sense that we are continuing a historical tradition.

These weavers enjoyed a relative abundance of materials. They could raise sheep for wool, grow flax for linen, and, from about the 19th century on, purchase ready-made cotton cloth. They could weave homespun for the household's daily use and purchase more finely woven cloth to make clothes for Sunday best. When those clothes wore out, they frugally made them into rugs so that they would get a second life.

Japanese weavers of sakiori faced something very different. Their use of rags in weaving emerged from an absolute lack of any other fibers beyond rough bast. As a result, their uses for the rag-woven cloth were more ubiquitous and creative. Their goal was not to frugally "use it up and wear it out" but to make a new cloth that retained all the desirable characteristics of the old.

Two approaches to rag weaving—one rooted in frugality, one in necessity—and together, a perfect approach to the historically unprecedented textile economy in which we now live. New textiles are abundant and cheap, but also wasteful, polluting, and sometimes accompanied by human rights abuses of textile workers.

As a result of the over-supply of cheap new textiles, thrift shops are overflowing with used textiles. Because clothing is manufactured quickly and cheaply, many of these items are not in good condition and cannot really be used for their original purpose. However, the fibers making up the cloth are the same as when they began life—silk, wool, cotton, rayon, and even polyester—and have the same basic properties.

I founded Western Sakiori to approach this new textile economy with the principle of frugality from my own North American tradition combined with the preservation of the original fiber properties from Japanese sakiori. It is a process that encourages conservation and creativity, and it is one that I hope other weavers will enjoy.

AMANDA ROBINETTE

Handwoven rag rugs for sale in the village of Kärdla on the island of Hiiumaa, Estonia, in northern Europe.

Why Rag Weaving?

Why weave with rags? With all the beautiful fibers, the indie dyers, and the locally grown sheep and alpaca, why do I choose to weave almost exclusively with rags? Here are some of my reasons, and maybe some of them will resonate with you as well.

To Make Beautiful Things

When we weave, we may have a particular goal in mind—a table needs a runner, the kitchen needs a new rug, we want yardage to make a new jacket—but no matter what we make, we want it to be beautiful. We want to enjoy the process of handling the warp yarn as we wind the warp and thread the loom. We like to see the warp threads as they line up on the warping reel or, as they lay across the warp beam, arranged into orderliness by the reed. Even the simplest of warps in the most

neutral of colors have a tactile and visual presence that we enjoy.

We watch the cloth begin to form, hoping that it will not reveal threading errors, delighting in the patterns and textures as they emerge at the fell line. Unless we are making an exact duplicate of something we have made many times, there is always at least a small moment of uncertainty—will it be as I imagined it?

I find that these experiences are heightened by weaving with rags. The used textiles that I find are always different

Busy prints and wild colors can, with the right warp, become beautiful rag weaving.

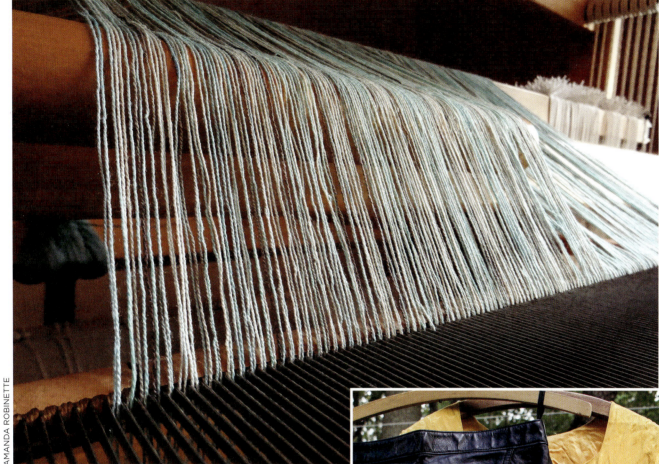

AMANDA ROBINETTE

Warping the loom is a tactile and visual pleasure.

in color, pattern, and type. The warp that is chosen will interact with those rags, sometimes in unexpected ways. No matter how many times I do it, I am never completely sure of the results until the cloth begins to appear and grow under my hands. Luckily, most rag weaving looks fantastic, no matter the warp choice or rag colors. It just works. And on the few occasions it does not, all you have to do is use a different rag that suits your warp better, and try something different next time with the original rag you chose. You really can't lose.

For the Joy of Creative Destruction

There is something oddly satisfying in taking things apart, especially if we are doing so to make something better from them. Refinishing furniture, removing old wallpaper to be able to paint a new color, unraveling an

Outdated styles are consigned to thrift shops and clothing recycling bins.

old sweater to re-use the yarn . . . the destruction is part of the creative process and should be enjoyed as such.

Many of the textiles that I take apart for rags have outlived their usefulness. They are old and tired-looking, or they might be perfect except for a large unremovable stain, or the material is great but the style is outdated or so strange that it wouldn't look good on anybody. It makes me feel good to turn something useless into something useful, and something ugly or unwieldy into something beautiful.

To Explore the Limits of Creativity

I often hear weavers wonder aloud what they should make next. And no wonder—in today's world, we can obtain any materials we want, from anywhere in the world. Weaving publications, books, and handweaving draft websites offer options so extensive, they might as well be limitless. It is unsurprising that sometimes weavers sound plaintive in their quest to decide on the next project—how can they decide between so many choices?

It might seem that unlimited choices would lead to unlimited creativity, but in my own weaving I have found the opposite to be true. Creativity actually flourishes when there is some adversity to be met or obstacle to overcome. This is the theory of creative limitation, as espoused by artist Phil Hansen, who said at a 2013 TED conference, "We need to first be limited in order to become limitless."

We have all heard the phrase "thinking outside the box," meaning that we need to think of unconventional and unexpected pathways to solutions instead of following the usual route. But, in order to think outside the box, we first have to get into the box, become one with the problem, and prioritize thinking our way out of it.

By placing limits on our weaving, we can actually fuel our own creativity. A weaver who limits herself to a rigid heddle loom will do far more with that loom than the weaver who also uses three floor looms. The first weaver will keep going further into her exploration of the rigid heddle loom, while the second will move on to the floor loom when she wants something different.

You will probably not want to dedicate most of your weaving time to rag weaving, as I have, but this principle can be applied one project at a time. By deciding to use rags to make something, you encounter obstacles. The best illustration of this is when we have some rags that we want to make into a project, but we don't want to make a rug. So, what do we do with those rags? Our minds get busy, thinking about possible projects, how to get the kind of fabric we want from the rags, what measures we should take to increase or decrease drape—all of the problem-solving decisions that really get our wheels turning. Before we know it, we have made sketches, done calculations, even considered sampling before we get started to make sure our idea will work. It is such an exciting process and the resulting project is completely our own, from start to finish.

To Be Environmentally Friendly

Many of us participate in recycling and make other choices to try to minimize our negative impact on the environment. Rag weaving can be seen as another step in the right direction. It accomplishes two things: first, by using old clothing, we keep it out of landfills and incinerators; second, it minimizes our consumption of new materials. I also feel that by using old textiles that no one wants anymore, I am honoring their original purpose and meaning. We live in a disposable culture. By rescuing something from that cycle, we show respect to the Earth, to the people who grew or made the fibers, and to the makers who turned it into a textile.

To Be Frugal

The costs of weaving add up. By the time we have bought the high-ticket items, like the loom, warping board or mill, shuttles and bobbins, bobbin winder, reeds, heddles, and on and on, we have made a huge investment. We want to use our equipment to make nice things, but fine yarn is expensive. If we weave with a rag weft, we only need to buy the warp yarn, and a little extra for some weft yarn picks. Even if we are buying our rags, they don't cost much at the thrift shop or yard sales, and a little bit goes a long way. Fine fibers like silk cost a lot less as rags than as cones of weaving yarn, so we can use better materials at less cost.

To Follow Tradition

During the long hours spent at the loom, many of us like to dwell on those who came before us. As our hands throw the shuttle and our feet step on the treadles, we feel a kinship with other hands and other feet engaged in the ages-old work of making cloth. By learning about the history of rag weaving in the world, both our corner of it and others, we can feel ourselves part of that tradition as well.

Turmeric-dyed white T-shirts and undershirts, on their way to a second life.

The History of Sakiori

The story of sakiori is most clearly viewed through the lens of a cold, forbidding world of high mountain peaks, steep valleys, and long, harsh winters. Narrow strips of land at the bottom of the valleys are cut through with precipitously descending rivers that turn into torrents during the spring thaw, flooding the fields of the farmers trying to eke out a living in the narrow land. Small fishing villages dot the coast where the rivers meet the sea, but are separated by the mountains from other nearby villages.

These scenes are especially characteristic of the yuki-guni—the "snow country" that lies at the northernmost end of Japan's main island of Honshu, in the Tohoku region. The common people living in this area were historically very poor and, even until the end of the 19th century for the inland communities, had little access to the outside world or trade goods. Because of this, they were among the last to give up the weaving and wearing of sakiori.

Japan is an archipelago lying in a northeast-to-southwest line 1,400 miles long between 200 and 500 miles off the east coasts of Russia, Korea, and China. Because of its far north–south reach and the high mountains covering 80 percent of the land, it has a wide variety of climates. Most of Japan has dry, cold winters and hot, humid summers. Okinawa, far to the south, has a subtropical climate, while Tohoku receives most of its precipitation in the winter, as snow.

The mountains made inland travel very difficult until modern times brought trains, roads, and airplanes. Many communities were fairly isolated, existing in the fringe between the mountains and the sea, or in narrow river valleys farther inland. In these individual villages, people had to use the resources that were available to them without the benefit of regular trade.

From the prehistory of the Jomon Period (8000–300 B.C.E.), civilization evolved in Japan from hunter-gatherer tribes into the feudal system of the Classical Period (710–1185 C.E.) and the Middle Ages (1185–1603 C.E.). During this time, 90 percent of the population lived on and worked the land for the *bushi* (warrior chieftains) as the peasant class.

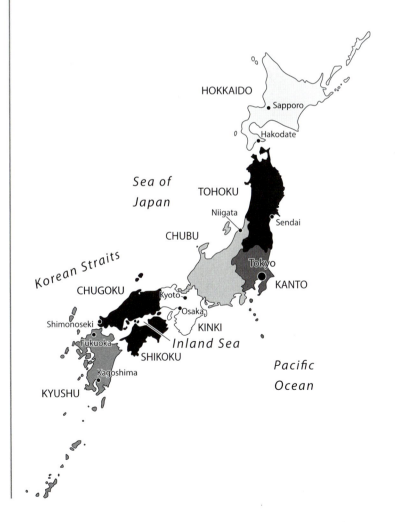

During the Middle Ages, a transition took place and feudal conditions gave way to land ownership for the common people. They were given cultivation rights but were subject to very difficult restrictions and suffered under a burdensome tax system. Population increase and land degradation led to a series of environmental disasters resulting in social crises and famine.

Throughout the Edo Period (1603–1868 C.E.), most Japanese continued to labor as farmers, foresters, or fishermen. A wealthy class flourished in Edo (now Tokyo), where there was much development of arts and culture.

During the Meiji Period (1868–1912 C.E.), Japan turned its focus outward, seeking to decide how to interact with the world at large. As part of this movement, Japan sought to join the Industrial Revolution already happening in Europe and North America.

The Modern Period (1912 C.E.–present) began with great change and turmoil, through the post–World War II Allied occupation, which finally ended in 1952. Japan then had a stable democratic government and a successful economy that allowed more of its people to enjoy the benefits of middle-class life. Today, Japan remains fully integrated into the current global economy and international relationships.

Native Bast Fibers in Japan

Since at least 8000 B.C.E., the common people of Japan made their cloth from the native bast fibers. As weavers, the bast fibers we are most familiar with are linen and perhaps hemp and ramie. Linen and ramie are highly valued for their luster, and all three are known for their strength, durability, and natural resistance to mold and mildew. We make clothing from these fibers when we want to stay cool and comfortable in the heat and wear something that the breeze can blow right through. These properties are very undesirable for anything but a warm summer's day, however, and we wisely change into cotton, wool, or silk (or, these days, synthetics) when we need a little added warmth. Unfortunately for the people living on the islands of Japan, none of these plant or animal sources was indigenous. Even linen and ramie, and possibly hemp, were not native to the Japanese islands. The Japanese had to be a bit more creative in their search for usable fiber for weaving.

The bast of a plant supports the layer of phloem (the vessels carrying nutrients through the stem down from the leaves) that lies between the bark or other outer wall of the stem and the inner, woodier core of xylem

(the vessels carrying water and nutrients up from the roots). It can be separated, often with a great deal of effort, from the other plant tissues to yield a fiber that can be spun or otherwise joined together into yarn. Native plants used in Japan for bast material include: wisteria, linden, elm, nettles, kudzu, paper mulberry, rose mallow, and arrowroot. In the far southern island of Okinawa, banana fiber was also often used. Hemp may also have been native to the Japanese islands, or may have been imported from China or Korea along with ramie (and, incidentally, silk, although this was reserved for the wealthy until modern times) around 300–200 B.C.E. It was at this time, as well, that weaving technology was brought to Japan.

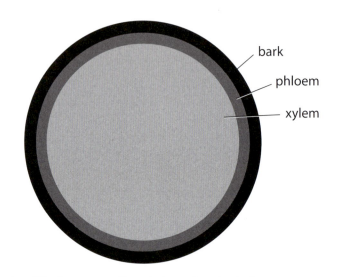

A simplified cross-sectional view of a plant stem. The bast fibers are in the phloem layer.

COURTESY OF SRI, BROOKLYN, NY; AMANDA ROBINETTE

Japanese bast fibers and cloth.

A much-mended sakiori garment.

PHOTOGRAPH COURTESY OF PRIVATE COLLECTION

Except for hemp, which was cultivated, and ramie, which could grow wild but was also cultivated, bast fibers had to be collected from where they grew in the forests and fields. This often entailed long and sometimes steep walks with heavy burdens. With trees like elm and paper mulberry, the layer between bark and wood was peeled and removed. Grasses and vines had to be cut and bundled. Back at home, the tree bast would be boiled with ash and then fermented to remove other material from the usable fiber, while the grasses and vines were retted—a process by which the outer layers are allowed or encouraged to decompose to free up the fibers.

Once the fibers were extracted, they were spun or, if very long, joined by knotting to make yarn for weaving. With certain exceptions, the fabric made from these bast fiber yarns was thick and tough, definitely meeting the requirement for durability in work garments. However, it wasn't good for keeping warm. People would wear as many layers as they had, but they were also forced to limit their outdoor activities on the most frigid days to avoid becoming dangerously cold.

Women were responsible for producing all of the textiles needed by their families. They gathered the bast, processed it into yarn, wove it into cloth, and sewed garments. This labor was accomplished during their "down time" from other responsibilities, such as childcare, farming, and cooking. Each piece of cloth and garment was highly valued due to the amount of labor required to produce it. Garments were mended and patched over and over again. They were sometimes disassembled to recover any usable cloth, which was patched and repaired until it made new yardage that could be re-sewn into a different garment. Women used sashiko, a type of running-stitch embroidery, to make their repairs, layer pieces together, and reinforce stress points on garments. Even small pieces of thread were saved to be used in mending or to be knotted together and used as weft for new cloth.

The reliance on native bast fibers continued, even as hemp and ramie cultivation became more common. Partly this was because hemp and ramie could not be grown in all of the regions of Japan. An onerous tax system was another reason. Hemp cloth was often used to pay taxes, and rural women would give over all of the hemp cloth they had produced in a year to meet the requirements. But it is also true that there were some occupations, such as forestry and fishing, for which the heavy native bast fabrics were better suited than finer cloth made from hemp or ramie.

The Arrival of Cotton

Cotton was imported to Japan from China and Korea as a luxury good in the 13th–15th centuries C.E. Even as trade increased and cotton became more common, it was still considered a high-value import, not something for common people to wear and use.

After Japan invaded Korea in 1592–1593 C.E., cotton cultivation was brought to the warmer areas of Japan. Theoretically, this should have made it less expensive and more available to commoners, but it continued as a highly prized and expensive fiber well into the Edo Period (1600–1868 C.E.). Also, like silk, in some parts of Japan it was reserved for the samurai class and was forbidden to everyone else.

By the end of the Edo Period, cotton cultivation had spread to most parts of Japan that were warm enough to support it, and it began to be available to commoners in those regions. However, new cotton fiber and cloth remained too expensive and was out of reach except for the wealthy and middle class. Farmers, fishermen, and other laborers could only afford used clothing or rags. In any case, government edicts often prohibited them from wearing new cotton cloth.

After generations of wearing bast fiber cloth, the common people during this time were enthusiastic about the softness and warmth of cotton—enthusiastic enough to use it in whatever condition they could obtain it. Used garments were patched and repaired, or taken apart to get pieces of relatively whole cloth that could be used for other purposes, or sewn together with other bits to make whole yardage. All of the same techniques that had been used to preserve their bast fiber garments were used to recycle and renew the used cotton they obtained through trade. Even in conservative rural communities, cotton became more common.

The Kitamaesen

In the colder areas in the north of Japan, cotton could not be grown and was only available through trade. During the Edo Period, the government developed a coastal shipping route, the western branch of which was called the Kitamaesen, to collect taxes from these regions and provide a means for trade with the more populated regions around the inland sea. Most taxes were collected in the form of rice, but in areas too cold for rice production, other goods like hemp cloth would be taken instead.

The ships of the Kitamaesen were small and designed to hug the coast, not venture into the ocean. They would travel from village to village, selling goods and collecting taxes. Besides goods like rice and fertilizer, they typically carried things like salt, pepper, sake, sugar, and cotton. The cotton trade was not an incidental one. For example, in the port of Niigata in 1697 C.E., cotton and used cotton were documented as second in value only to rice and other grains.

Used cotton, purchased by merchants in cotton-growing areas, was bundled together into a tabane-tsugi (bale of rags), each composed of 20–24 kg (44–52 pounds) of dirty and damaged cloth. A group of villagers along the Kitamaesen would team up to buy one tabane to share. As it was typically filthy, the

The Kitamaesen route passed through the Inland Sea to the west coast of Japan and reached areas far to the north.

first thing to be done was to scour the cloth. Next, it would be sorted by quality. The highest-quality fabrics (noshi-tsugi) were the largest and most complete pieces, reserved for making underwear, being sewn into sashiko cloth, or pieced together as futon covers. The lowest-quality scraps (sagi) were used for sakiori.

Sakiori

Some form of rag weaving had likely been practiced by Japanese peasants before the availability of cotton rags, given the precious nature of cloth. It was not prevalent, however, which makes sense because the amount of cloth required for rag weaving is more than a single household was likely to have available. With the advent of trade in cotton rags, however, sakiori became a normal wardrobe component.

Women used the same loom for sakiori that they used to make bast fiber cloth. This was the jibata ("loom that sits on the ground"), a type of modified backstrap loom brought to Japan from Korea or China around the 5th century. It consists of a backstrap loom inside a frame with a lifter attached to the weaver's foot for changing sheds and a batten for beating. Over time, weavers added a reed (osa) to organize the warp threads and a batten that also acted as a shuttle.

The jibata is ideal for weaving bast fiber cloth because the backstrap tensioning allows the weaver to use less tension than a frame loom and make a more elastic cloth from the stiff bast fibers. When women began weaving sakiori, they added a heavier batten to their toolkit so they could firmly beat the rags into place, and increased the tension while beating.

Sakiori was considered to be fast weaving, partly because of the thick weft but also because it minimized the use of bast fibers, which were very laborious to prepare. Modern weavers probably have a different opinion about how fast it is to prepare and weave with narrow rag strips as opposed to throwing a boat shuttle with a mechanically wound bobbin carrying purchased yarn!

Once scoured and sorted, the rags chosen for sakiori were torn or cut with a knife or scissors into strips. The width of the strips varied according to local custom and the intended use of the cloth, but they were generally about a tenth of an inch (3 mm) wide. Most of the cotton cloth would have been dyed with indigo, either patterned or plain. Later in the 19th and 20th centuries C.E., modern industrial dyes became more common, and these more colorful rags were often saved for special garments or items like obi that would be highly visible when worn.

After the rags were prepared, the jibata would be warped with bast fiber, preferably hemp (cotton yarn came into use later as it became less expensive). It was

Two examples of mid-20th-century sakiori. On the right is material for making a sodenashi; on the left is an obi. Note the differences between sakiori made for a work versus a decorative garment.

warped either full-width (namihaba), about 13–14 in (33–36 cm), or half-width (hanhaba). The half-width cloth was for making children's clothing or sleeveless vests (sodenashi) for work.

Traditional Japanese clothing is minimally tailored. The cloth is used as it comes from the loom, in rectangular shape, and the garment is formed by folding and sewing these pieces together. This was especially true of the bast fiber cloth and sakiori made by Japanese peasants, who had every reason not to waste it or weaken the cloth by cutting and trimming. If adjustments for fit needed to be made, these were done by adding flat cotton gussets, collars, and trim, which could be replaced

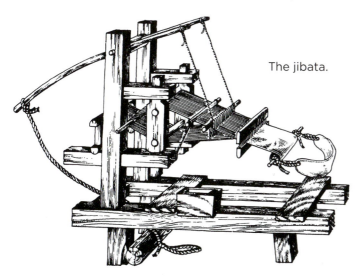

The jibata.

Two Japanese women weaving; the loom on the right is a jibata.

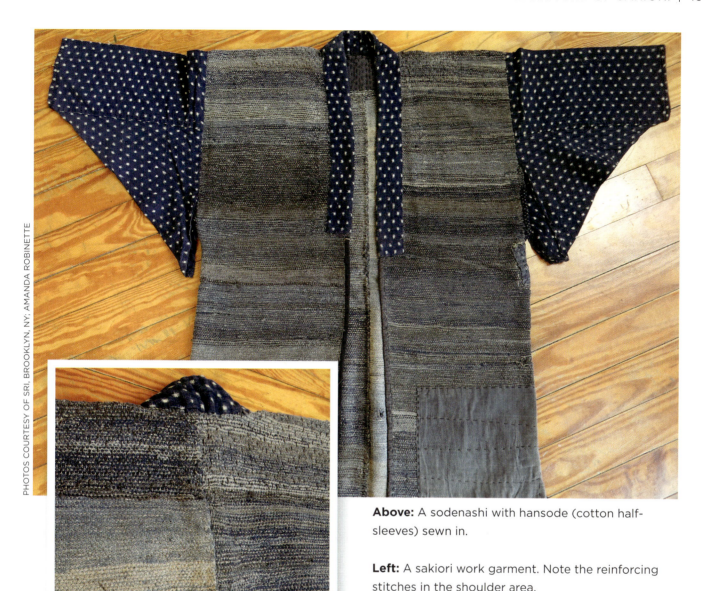

Above: A sodenashi with hansode (cotton half-sleeves) sewn in.

Left: A sakiori work garment. Note the reinforcing stitches in the shoulder area.

when worn or removed if the cloth was going to be remade into a garment for a different use or person.

Sakiori garments provided warmth, comfort, and durability to farmers, foresters, and fishermen, as well as a reduction in labor for the women who did the spinning, weaving, and sewing. Women also engaged in outdoor manual labor, such as planting rice and hauling timber, and wore sakiori for these tasks. Garments were made to suit the work of the person wearing them. For example, women planting rice would wear sodenashi with cotton half-sleeves (hansode) sewn into the armholes. These provided some protection from sunburn but were not long enough to get muddy. Fishermen and foresters wore aprons (maegake) to protect their clothes from being

soaked or torn up by brush, respectively. Garments worn by those carrying burdens would have sashiko stitching in the upper back or wherever a strap would fall to reinforce and protect the fabric.

By the mid-20th century C.E., Japan had become a modernized nation intent upon embracing the global future and forgetting the impoverished past. As the economy changed and the population shifted to urban centers, sakiori gradually became associated with an outmoded and old-fashioned way of life. Fortunately, some Japanese weavers kept the knowledge alive, and today there is a new generation of weavers and fiber artists who use sakiori to remember the past and to envision a new future.

Opposite page: A Japanese woman weaving.

Getting Started

There are some special considerations that make weaving with rags somewhat different from weaving with yarn. For one thing, the rag weft is often significantly heavier than the warp threads, meaning that the result is not a balanced weave: there will be more ends to the inch in the warp than picks per inch in the weft. The heavier weft can make the fabric heavy and stiff as well, but certain measures can be taken to minimize this effect. Calculating draw-in of the warp width and take-up in the length can also vary from typical weaving. It is even more crucial in rag weaving

to consider very carefully how you would like the end product to feel and how structured you want it to be.

All about Rags

Finding and Selecting Rags

The most important principle in choosing what type of rag to use is what properties you want the finished cloth to have. If you want the piece to have a lot of drape, look for fabrics woven of fine threads, such as silk or cotton gauze. Even among silks, you can differentiate

A selection of silk rags.

AMANDA ROBINETTE

A rag weaver's palette of color and fiber.

How to Shop at Thrift Stores
(a primer for the uninitiated)

When I was growing up, thrift stores were decidedly un-cool. People usually shopped there by necessity, not choice, and many of the things for sale were worn out. However, circumstances have changed, drastically. Fast fashion and cheap shopping opportunities have created such an excess of textiles that today's thrift shops are bursting at the seams with textiles, many of which are new or barely worn, and very few of which are in actual deplorable condition. Mostly, they are there because of changing styles and the overflowing closets of our society. Often, if something is damaged, it is very slight, such as a small hole or stain, or a missing button. Thrift stores tend to organize their clothing by gender, then type, then color (or, sometimes, by size, then color). For example, the T-shirts in the "Men's T-shirts" section are grouped into swaths of red, orange, blue, green, and so on.

Nothing could be more convenient for us weavers bent on bringing our project idea to life. You can go straight to the fabric weight desired (lighter in women's blouses, dresses, and skirts, slightly heavier in men's shirts and bed sheets, heaviest in pants), find the color you want, and skim the rack for the fiber content that you are seeking. If you love the treasure-hunt aspects of thrift shopping, it is a fun adventure. If you don't, it is, at worst, an efficient process.

Getting Started: Tools and Equipment for Rag Weaving

Equipment needed for rag weaving:

- A weaving loom that makes at least two sheds (a two-harness floor or table loom or a rigid heddle loom) and the warping equipment needed for the loom
- Boat or stick shuttle for carrying the weft yarn, and bobbins and a bobbin winder if needed for shuttle
- Rag or stick shuttle for carrying rag weft
- Sharp fabric scissors
- Seam ripper
- Tape measure, T-pins, and other weaving equipment as preferred by the individual weaver
- Empty cones or other weighting system for adding floating selvedges

Other equipment you may want to use:

- Rotary cutter, guide, and mat
- Rag cutter
- Weaving temple
- Dust mask
- Supplementary beater/weaving sword (for rigid heddle loom)
- Fringe twister
- Sewing machine

between thicker satin or brocade weaves and very thin plain weave. If you are planning a sturdy tote bag, then a more coarsely woven cloth can be a good choice. The bottom line is that you won't get properties out of the woven fabric that you don't put into it—a soft cotton will not feel like a cool, smooth silk no matter what weave structure or warp thread you use. A silk blouse that has a "crunchy" feel or has become dull from age or cleaning chemicals will not get silkier or shinier from being rag-woven. When selecting items to use as rags, feel them, see how they drape, and examine their luster.

Rags can come from any textiles, from garments to old sheets, and from sources as eclectic as prom dresses and leather upholstery. If you can cut it or tear it, you can turn it into weft. The sky's the limit!

There are two possible starting points for rag weaving projects: the rags or the finished object. In the first case, the weaver has some rags that they want to use, but no set idea of what to make. For example, a pile of blanket sleepers that has been kept because of fond memories of cuddling the babies wearing them, or a few favorite blouses that were worn until they became unusable due to stains or holes but could not be parted with. Under these circumstances, the weaver should look at the items and determine their dominant properties. Colorful, thin, and flowing might just equal a scarf or shawl. Thick and fleecy might tend toward a cushy bath mat. A medium-weight cotton might make a nice structured jacket.

The opposite approach is to decide what to make, and then go looking for the rags needed to make it. In this case, the hunt might lead you to one of my favorite places . . . the THRIFT STORE (see p. 15)!

Preparing Rags for Weaving

All textiles should be washed before weaving with them, even those marked dry-clean only. You are almost always going to wet-finish the piece after weaving, so it is important to get any color bleeding or shrinkage out of the way beforehand. It is also a good way to cut down on dust and loose threads, as well as removing potential contaminants of stored textiles like mold or insect casings. Not to mention that people do not always wash their clothes before donating them!

If you know that you will be machine-washing the finished object, machine-wash the textiles first. If you are going to put it in the dryer, and the fibers are subject to shrinkage, then dry the textiles you will use for rags

A word to the wise: To avoid bringing home anything unexpected in your thrift shop goods, keep them in a plastic bag outside of your house—in the trunk of your car, in the garage, or on the porch or balcony—until you are ready to wash them. For items you do not intend to wash, like a leather jacket that is not in need of a professional cleaning, hang outside for several days in the sun, if possible, or, in the winter, leave outside to freeze. Turn inside out and shake well, visually inspecting the seams and pockets. You can also place them in your car parked in the sun on a hot summer day, so the intense heat can do its job. I prefer not to bring unwashed items into the house until there has been a hot, sunny day to heat-treat, even if it means waiting all winter! Isn't that what garages are for?

as well. On rare occasions, such as the Wedding Dress Bed Runner project (p. 80), the final piece is intended to be dry-clean only, and there is no reason to wet-finish to soften the woven piece because it should be a more structured item as opposed to a wearable. In these cases, it is not necessary to wash the rag textiles (although it may still be desirable, depending on their condition!).

Creative Destruction

Once your textiles are clean and ready to process, they need to be deconstructed to make it easier to cut them into strips. For garments, you will first want to reduce them into their original pattern pieces. Often, it is

Carefully trimming the rolled hems allows you to use them for other purposes.

I throw out the seams from deconstructed garments, but I like to cut neatly along the edge of the rolled hems and save them. The stitching keeps them from coming apart and they can be braided together and used for button loops, bracelets, or tie closures.

A fun bracelet made from silk rolled hems.

Remove and save the buttons!

best to just cut away rolled hems and seams entirely, because the amount of fabric that you save by using a seam ripper to cut these open is tiny compared to the effort required. Also, the fabric that was sewn into the seam is often quite damaged from the sewing stitches and can be unusable.

Remove the buttons and cut away any fabric that has fused interfacing applied. Over the years, I have saved all of the buttons from my rag weaving, and my button box now boasts an impressive collection in all colors, shapes, and sizes. I will never need to buy buttons again!

Once the garment has been reduced to flat pieces, you can prepare your strips for weaving.

Tearing vs. Cutting

Traditional sakiori was made using either of these methods of making strips. Which one you use is up to your personal preference and the characteristics of the fabric. Plain weave and some pattern weaves may be suitable for tearing. It is easy to check. Cut a slit about two inches long on one edge of the fabric and then try to tear it. If it tears neatly along a straight line, you can keep cutting slits and tearing from that side. If it doesn't seem to want to tear evenly (or at all), try cutting a slit on an adjacent edge and tearing. Some cloth will tear easily in either the warp or the weft direction, while some only tears in one direction or the other. Complex weaves will generally not tear in a straight line under any circumstances, and must be cut.

There are many different ways to cut your strips. You can, of course, just use a pair of scissors and a cutting board, but this is the most time-consuming and least

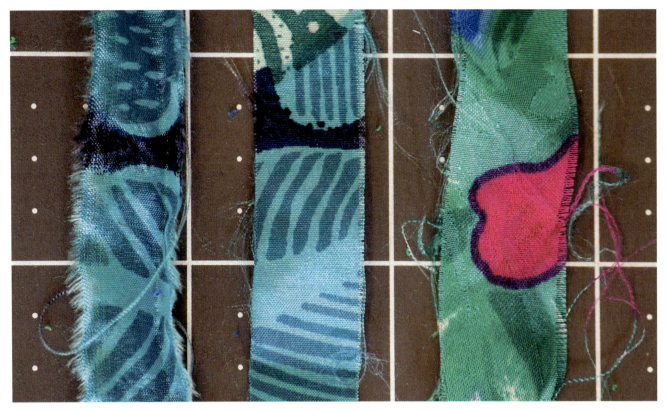

Left, Plain-weave silk strip made by tearing. *Center,* The same silk cut with a rag-cutter. *Right,* silk brocade (complex weave) cut with a rag cutter. Note the threadiness of the brocade fabric even though a cutter is used.

Check if your fabric will tear easily. If tearing works for your fabric, it is a good idea to cut your slits a little wider than you want the strips to be, because they will come out a little narrower after tearing due to the fuzzing of the torn area.

exact way. A rotary cutter, cutting mat, and a clear cutting guide work very well, producing even strips with less strain on your hands. You can also use these tools to cut your fabric in a continuous strip if you are not changing rags or if you want wide stripes in the weft.

My favorite way to cut rag strips is to use my Fraser Rag Cutter. I have an adjustable blade on mine so that I can cut any width I would like from ½ in to 2 in (1.3 cm to 5 cm) wide. It is easy and ergonomic to use because you just feed the fabric through with one hand and turn the crank with the other. There are also various electric fabric strip cutters, available at fabric and craft stores. I prefer the hand crank because it allows more control, especially when dealing with thin silk.

If you are cutting tubular fabric, such as T-shirts or felted sweaters, you can obtain a continuous strip by

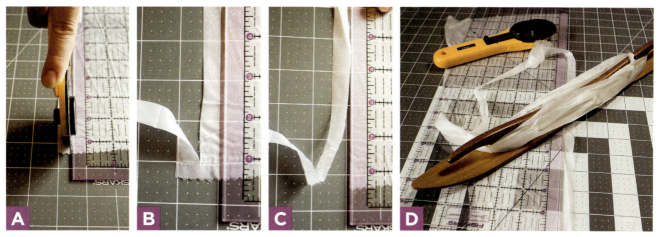

Continuous Strip Method: A - Cut to about ½ in (1.3 cm) of edge; **B** - Move guide over to make next cut; **C** - Begin next cut from uncut edge to form continuous strip; **D** - This method allows you to fill a shuttle with a continuous strip, making for much faster weaving.

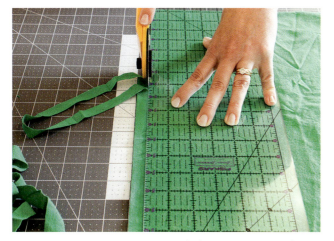

Using a rotary cutter, mat, and clear cutting guide results in clean cuts and consistent sizing.

Continuous strip method: Begin at one edge (X) and cut to ½ in (1.3 cm) from the opposite edge (Y). Move guide and, beginning at the opposite edge (Y), cut to within ½ in (1.3 cm) of the first edge (X). Repeat, alternating which edge is cut all the way through. You can trim the corners as you go or while winding your rag shuttle to help them lie flat in the shed.

Cutting strips with the rag cutter is easy and fast.

cutting with scissors in a spiral up from the hem edge until you reach the bottom of the armholes (see the Rustic Wool Hearth Rug and Log Carrier project, p. 64).

For knitwear like T-shirts, you could also cut loops and join them as described in the Walking on Sunshine T-shirt Rug project (p. 64).

Deciding on a Warp Yarn

Your choice of warp yarn is another determining factor in the type of cloth you will weave. The properties of the warp yarn will be preserved in the final product just like those of the rags. To enhance drape and softness, use a cellulose warp, such as rayon, tencel, or bamboo. For something sturdy and structured, carpet warp or bast fibers, such as linen or hemp, are ideal. For durability with more softness, perle cotton is a good choice.

Consider how your warp yarn will interact with your rags when making your decision. A tencel warp can make thin cotton rag soft and flowing, but will not be able to substantially change a heavy cotton canvas. Thin

Warp yarns.

silk shirting is not a very durable material and not well suited for heavy use, so it doesn't make a lot of sense to use carpet warp to weave it.

Planning the Project

Traditional sakiori was woven in plain weave with cotton rag and a warp of hemp or another bast fiber, normally with one pick of rag alternating with two picks of the warp yarn as weft. Adding picks of the warp yarn made the fabric more pliable and allowed for more yardage from whatever cotton rag was available. Why two picks of warp yarn? Remember that the Japanese woman weaving sakiori had a two-harness loom, and thus two sheds only (let's call them A and B). If she put rag in shed A, hemp yarn in shed B, and rag again in shed A, she would end up with a fabric that looked like it had vertical stripes of rag weft. To get the look and consistency of a plain weave fabric, the weft rag must lie in alternating sheds. By weaving rag in shed A, hemp in shed B, hemp in shed A, and then rag in shed B, she achieves that effect.

Factors such as take-up, draw-in, sett, and more are different for rag weaving than for other weave structures. Additionally, the rag produced by each fabric is unique, as is the way each weaver weaves. Because of this, if your

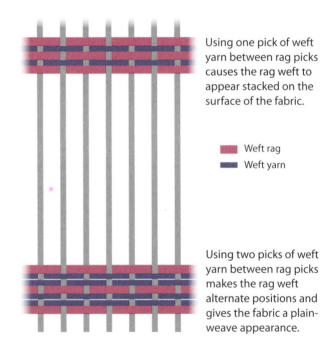

Using one pick of weft yarn between rag picks causes the rag weft to appear stacked on the surface of the fabric.

■ Weft rag
■ Weft yarn

Using two picks of weft yarn between rag picks makes the rag weft alternate positions and gives the fabric a plain-weave appearance.

rags are from special textiles, or if you need a project to be an exact measurement, sampling is in order.

You can use the Sakiori Sett Chart (p. 22) to plan your projects, or as a starting point for your sampling. The warp threads will be sett at fewer ends per inch than for balanced weave structures. I have listed here the warp yarns that I use most often and the setts that work for me.

Sakiori Weaving Worksheet

Project Description: _____

Warp Yarn #1: _____

Manufacturer: _____

Colorway, Dye Lot: _____

Weight, Yd/lb: _____

Warp Yarn #2: _____

Manufacturer: _____

Colorway, Dye Lot: _____

Weight, Yd/lb: _____

Weft Rags: _____

_____

Strip Width: _____

Weft Yarn: _____

Manufacturer: _____

Colorway, Dye Lot: _____

Weight, Yd/lb: _____

For ends per inch (EPI), refer to the Sakiori Sett Chart (p. 22), or use slightly fewer than half of the wraps per inch (wpi) for that yarn (i.e., sett a yarn with 48 wpi at 20 EPI.).

Picks per inch (PPI) = The number of picks of that type of weft only that are in each inch. Roughly, this is equal to about one-quarter of the wraps per inch for that material.

WARP CALCULATIONS

Sett: _____ EPI (ends per inch)

Desired finished width: _____ inches

Add 15% of width: + _____ inches

Equals **Total Width**: = _____ inches

Total Width: _____ inches

Multiply by Sett: x _____ EPI

Equals **Total Ends**: = _____ warp ends

Desired finished length: _____ inches

Add 7% of length: + _____ inches

Hem/Fringes: + _____ inches

Equals **Project Length**: = _____ inches

Add loom waste (20–30 in): + _____ inches

Equals warp length (inches): = _____ inches

Divide by 36 inches: ÷ 36 inches

Equals **Warp Length (yards)**: = _____ yards

Total Ends: _____ warp ends

Multiply by Warp Length (yards):

                      x _____ yards

Equals Yards of Warp Yarn Required:

                      = _____ yards

WEFT CALCULATIONS

Weft Yarn:

Picks per inch (PPI):   _____ picks

Total Width of warp: _____ inches

Multiply by PPI: x _____ picks

Multiply by Project Length: x _____ inches

Equals weft yarn required (inches):

                        = _____ inches

Divide by 36 inches: ÷ 36 inches

Equals Weft Yarn Required (yards): = _____ yards

Weft Rag:

Picks per inch (PPI):   _____ picks

Total Width of warp: _____ inches

Multiply by PPI: x _____ picks

Multiply by Project Length: x _____ inches

Equals weft rag required (inches): = _____ inches

Divide by 36 inches: ÷ 36 inches

Equals Weft Rag Required (yards): = _____ yards

Sakiori Sett Chart

Fiber	Yarn (yards/lb)	Sett for plain weave (ends per inch)
Bamboo	Bambu 7 (Silk City) (2,100)	12
	Bambu 12 (Silk City) (6,300)	20
	8/2 (3,360)	16
Cotton	20/2 (8,400)	30
	10/2 (8,475)	20
	8/2 (6,775)	16
	8/4 carpet warp (1,600)	12–16
Tencel	Laceweight (2,520)	12
	8/2 (3,360)	16
	10/2 (4,200)	20
Soysilk	Laceweight (6,370)	16

Similarly, the Sakiori Weaving Worksheet (p. 21) takes into account the typical draw-in (weft-wise) and take-up (warp-wise) of sakiori. In the worksheet, I use the average draw-in (15 percent) and take-up (7 percent) that I have experienced in weaving projects with finely cut rags, such as the scarf projects in this book. Projects with heavier weft will yield different results, such as less draw-in and more take-up. With very heavy wefts, such as 1-inch felted sweater strips, the finished width will actually exceed the width of the warp in the reed.

How Much Do I Need?

This is the most common question among new rag weavers. The answer is a resoundingly unsatisfying, "It depends." On the Sakiori Weaving Worksheet, you will see that there is a place to estimate rag yardage needed. However, weavers don't usually know how many yards of rag they have. If you are weaving with old clothes and other used textiles, you may know that you have three men's dress shirts or six girls' dresses, but that doesn't tell you how many feet you will be able to weave on a warp 8 in (20 cm) wide.

There is no hard and fast rule. The answer depends on so many factors. How wide are your fabric strips? How much does each textile yield? How firmly are you beating the cloth? How wide is your warp?

The answers are only obtained via two routes (outside of actual sampling): guesswork and experience. The projects in this book can give you a place to start. To be on the safe side while you are learning, I recommend choosing some extra textiles for your rag weft, and weaving in hit-or-miss fashion with all of the different colors and patterns from the beginning. That way you won't run out of your rags when you need to weave another foot on your project.

If you need certain results, then you should certainly sample! All amounts given in project instructions are approximate.

Special Considerations in Weaving

Tension

Good rag weaving requires high tension and a firm beat. Many of the warp yarns used in the projects in this book are not typically placed under high tension. For example, tencel is supposed to be woven under lighter tension because it is prone to shredding and breaking under the stress of high tension. However, for use as a warp yarn in sakiori, the warp should be tighter.

> The jibata loom, with its backstrap tensioning, allowed the weaver to reduce the tension enough to get a good shed and to raise the tension to get a firm beat, simply by leaning back and forth. (See illustration on p. 11.)

How high should your warp thread tension be while weaving? Of course, it is difficult to describe in writing, but I always imagine the military rule: would a quarter bounce on the warp threads? (Soldiers are told to make a bed so tightly that a quarter will bounce off of it.) Your hand should be able to bounce the warp threads slightly (less than 1/2 in [1.3 cm]), and they should feel tight. Based on seeing my students try to tension their looms, you should tension the loom like you normally would, and then crank it one or two more clicks. If you are having trouble opening a shed, then it is too tight.

Weaving yarns like tencel and bamboo under this high tension can certainly lead to problems. These are the methods I successfully use to minimize the stress on my warp threads:

* After spreading the warp with waste yarn for at least an inch, place a floating selvedge on each side. Pin the floating selvedge end to the waste yarn, thread it through the first open dent in the reed on that side, and hang it off the back beam with a weight *without* threading it into a heddle. When weaving, always go *over* the floating selvedges when throwing the shuttle from right to left, and *under* them when going from left to right.

* As soon as you have enough woven material to accommodate it, begin using a temple. Temples come in widths as small as 6–8 in (15–20 cm) to work with

When weaving, always go *over* the floating selvedges when throwing the shuttle from right to left, and *under* them when going from left to right.

A selection of temples.

AMANDA ROBINETTE

The temple spreads the warp threads so that they come straight from the reed to the fell line.

most narrow warps, and the Leclerc Clip Temple can be used with any width warp. A temple is used to spread the woven cloth right at the fell line to the width of the warp in the reed. It is not designed to reduce actual draw-in in the final cloth, but rather to keep the warp threads running in a straight line from the fell to the reed. This produces a more even and firm beat and reduces the stress that typically occurs on the warp threads at the selvedges.

Broken warp threads do sometimes happen, even when taking these precautions. If you are getting a lot of broken threads, consider the following possibilities. Is your tension too tight? Try loosening it a little. Is your warp yarn old, or is it a certain color that keeps breaking? Sometimes a yarn just goes bad, whether from age, dye stress, or sun exposure. Does your reed have any rust or pitting inside the dents? These areas can cause excessive wear on warp threads. Are you allowing enough weft in each pick to accommodate the draw-in? Make sure you are placing the weft in the shed at an angle and not pulling it tightly across or holding it tight while beating.

Draw-in still occurs when using a temple, but note that it does not happen at the fell line, where it can stress and weaken the selvedge warp threads.

Rag Weaving on a Rigid Heddle Loom

Successful rag weaving requires high tension and a firm beat, two things that are difficult to achieve on a rigid heddle loom. However, with a few modifications, it is possible to weave beautiful sakiori pieces with your rigid heddle loom. Here are a few things to keep in mind:

- The sett that you can achieve is limited by the rigid heddle itself. You may need to choose heavier yarns than most of those used in the projects for this book. For example, instead of 8/2 (3,360 yd/lb) or 10/2 (4,200 yd/lb) tencel, you can use laceweight tencel (2,520 yd/lb), which can be sett at 12 EPI with a 12-dent rigid heddle for plain rag weave. You can use the Sakiori Weaving Worksheet (p. 21) to calculate your warp with the sett you will use.

A rigid heddle loom.

- Rigid heddle looms do not typically work well with warps that are longer than 3 yd (2.7 m). The cloth beam also fills up quickly, so if you are making several items at once, you may need to keep cutting them off and re-tying the warp. If you are trying to weave with heavy rag, the project will necessarily need to be shorter than what it could be on a floor loom.

- There are limits to how high you can crank the tension on a rigid heddle loom without damaging the loom. To avoid this, adjust the tension to higher than you would normally put it, but not so high that you can feel the warp threads straining the warp and/or cloth beam. There will be more give to the warp threads than as described for floor looms, and the resulting cloth will generally be looser and less tightly woven.

- To get a firm beat, use a supplemental beater with a beveled edge, such as a belt shuttle or weaving sword. Use it to firmly press, rather than strike, the rags or weft yarn into place. Weave in the following rhythm: place pick, change shed, beat with supplementary beater, and repeat.

- It is easier to get proper tension and a firm beat on a narrower piece on the rigid heddle loom.

Firmly press the rag weft into place with a beveled-edge supplementary beater.

Use the floating selvedge to make a neat turn with your rag weft.

Sakiori Wet-Finishing Guide

Warp Yarn	Rag Fiber Type	Washing	Drying
Cellulose fibers: tencel, bamboo, rayon, etc.; azlon (soysilk)	Silk, rayon, cotton (pre-shrunk), linen	Warm water, mild detergent, delicate cycle	Low or extra-low heat with a large towel, no fabric softener, check every 20 minutes
Cotton; bast fibers	Silk, rayon, cotton, linen	Cold water, mild detergent, delicate cycle	Hang to dry or tumble on air dry only (no heat)
Any fiber	Polyester, nylon, plastics, etc.	Cold water, mild detergent, delicate cycle	Hang to dry or tumble on air dry only (no heat)

* Weave in the following rhythm: Open the shed, throw the shuttle, beat, change the shed with beater forward, and beat again. Repeat. Beating on an open shed and changing sheds with the beater at the fell reduces stress on the selvedge warp threads, and beating twice produces a firmer, more even fabric.

Other Weaving Considerations

* To minimize bulk at the selvedges, begin a new yarn end or rag by cutting away half of the rag width or unplying and cutting away half the plies of the weft yarn for a length of about 3 in (7.5 cm). Overlap the narrower sections at the selvedge so that the total bulk is the same as the rest of the weft.
* Similarly, when overlapping ends in the shed, remove half of the weft width and overlap the narrower ends so the pick is the same all the way across.
* Decide before you begin if you would like to have a hem or a fringe. If a fringe is desired, don't forget to leave a length of warp yarn at the beginning and end of your piece for it.
* You can keep your selvedges neat by using your fingers to place the weft in the shed at the selvedge, pulling it against the floating selvedge so that no loop is left. However, don't forget to allow plenty of give for the weft across the rest of the warp by laying it in at an angle.

Finishing

Most sakiori should be wet-finished, particularly if it is intended for wearing. Wet-finishing relaxes and softens natural fibers, and agitation allows fibers to slide around each other and even out in the warp and weft, making your weaving look more finished. For cellulose fibers like rayon, tencel, and bamboo, machine-washing and drying have a magical effect, changing cloth from stiff to fluid in one fell swoop. Ironing also helps this process along and is a chance to even out ends and square up corners.

Be sure to follow the finishing instructions for each project in this book. If you substitute a warp yarn or weft rag fiber, you will want to follow the instructions in the Sakiori Wet-Finishing Guide above for what you used.

Some projects specify no wet-finishing, or that it is unnecessary. In those cases, it is desirable for the fabric to have more structure than softness, or the project has been constructed or embellished to the extent that it should only be dry-cleaned.

THE
Projects

BEGINNING WITH THE BASICS: SCARVES AND SAMPLING

MAKING MEMORIES

FOR THE HOME

WEAVING TO WEAR

Beginning with the Basics
SCARVES AND SAMPLING

Many weavers, like knitters, make a lot of scarves when they are learning their craft. Scarves are narrow, don't take a lot of materials, and provide a long length on which to learn a new technique or sample with specific fiber choices. For sakiori, they also serve as an excellent example of how much drape can be achieved in rag weaving when we push the boundaries of the expected.

AMANDA ROBINETTE

Basic Western Sakiori Scarf

This is a beginner's project that I use for teaching sakiori. It is a good way to get started and produces something students can take home to wear and impress their friends and family! Silk is an excellent material for a rag scarf. When mixed with a warp of bamboo, tencel, or other rayon-type cellulose warps, it creates a supple, flowing material that wraps elegantly around the neck. Silk is warm and insulating without being fuzzy or rustic-looking. You could use other types of rag in your sakiori scarf, but with the beautiful colors and patterns of silk available, why would you?

This scarf is woven traditionally, with one pick of fine-cut rags alternating with two picks of the warp yarn. The rag came from two different ladies' blouses, one dark teal and one with purple, yellow, and green stripes. The teal shirt was a heavy silk satin while the striped shirt was a thin plain weave silk. To compensate for the difference in weight, I cut the heavier silk a little thinner, around ³⁄₈ in (.9 cm). I alternated strips from each shirt to make an irregularly striped scarf and used the same variegated tencel in both warp and weft.

Materials

Warp: 8/2 tencel (3,360 yd/lb), Valley Yarns, Jewel Combo, 378 yd (345 m)

Weft yarn: Same as warp yarn, 212 yd (194 m)

Weft rags: Lightweight silk from two women's blouses, cut into $\frac{1}{2}$-in (1.3-cm) or $\frac{3}{8}$-in (.9-cm) strips (see above) (approximately 106 yd [97 m] of strips)

Warping and Weaving

Sett: 16 EPI (2 ends per dent in an 8-dent reed)

Weave structure: Plain weave

Width in reed: 7.75 in (19.7 cm)

Wind a 3-yd (2.75-m) warp of 124 ends and warp your loom by your desired method. Set up the loom for plain weave. After allowing at least 8 in (20 cm) of warp yarn for fringe, weave a header of at least an inch with waste yarn to spread the warp and provide an anchor for adding floating selvedges and a place to secure a temple. If desired, begin with leaving a 24-in (61-cm) weft yarn tail for hemstitching.

Under high tension, weave in plain weave, beginning with six picks of weft yarn only and then alternating one pick of weft rag with two picks of weft yarn. Weave for 70 in (178 cm) or to the desired length, finishing with six picks of weft yarn, and hemstitching, if desired. Secure with 1 in (2.5 cm) of waste yarn, and cut from loom, allowing at least 8 in (20 cm) for fringe.

Finishing

Finished dimensions: $6\frac{2}{3}$ in (17 cm) x 62 in (157.5 cm), excluding fringe

Finish fringe as desired. Twisting or braiding is recommended to keep the fine yarns from tangling and fraying in washing and wearing the scarf.

Follow wet-finishing instructions for **tencel warp/silk rag** on page 27. Machine-dry with a large towel on low or no heat, checking every 20 minutes, until dry. Using an iron set on low to medium, hard press with steam, using iron to square up corners and straighten ends.

Care

Hand wash in cold water with mild detergent or shampoo. Rinse well and spin water out in washing machine set on spin or in a salad spinner. Dry and press as for **Finishing**.

AMANDA ROBINETTE

AMANDA ROBINETTE

4 Harness Loom
Threading and Tie-Up

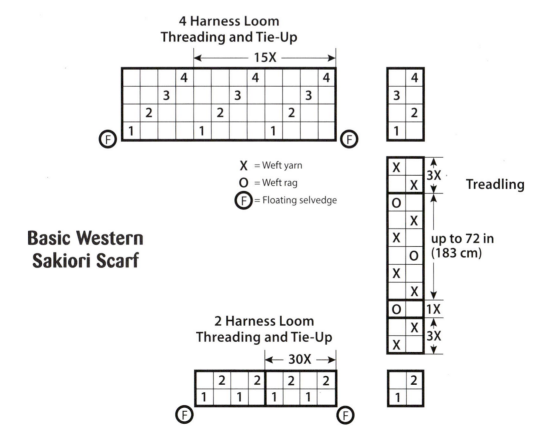

15X

X = Weft yarn
O = Weft rag
F = Floating selvedge

Treadling

up to 72 in
(183 cm)

3X

1X

3X

Basic Western
Sakiori Scarf

2 Harness Loom
Threading and Tie-Up

30X

Bright Bamboo Scarf

Bamboo is another favorite warp yarn. Like tencel, it results in a fabric with superb drape. It is available in many colors and can also be purchased undyed to make your own unique colorway.

I like to use a black warp for very colorful rags to frame and set off the colors. These rags came from one of the great thrift shop mysteries that I regularly encounter—the silk shorts-set. It is sister to another great mystery, the silk tracksuit. They often come in appalling colors and prints and usually show signs of not having been worn very often. Over the years I have pondered these items, and I still do not understand them. Thin silk shorts and pants seem like a bad idea altogether, and a matching loud print on the top and the bottom overwhelms any figure. For such a casual or sporty outfit to be made of silk also confuses the mind. Is the tracksuit intended for something like a spa day, as something to change into for lunch or drinks in the lounge between treatments? Perhaps the shorts-set is sold under that strange category, cruise-wear, suited for that and little else?

We may never know the answers to these mysteries, but we can take advantage of the garish prints and loud colors to make a vibrant scarf to brighten our winter days.

Materials

Warp: Bambu 7 (2,100 yd/lb), Silk City Fibers, Onyx 360, 324 yd (300 m)

Weft yarn: Same as warp yarn, 228 yd (208 m)

Weft rags: Lightweight silk from shirt and shorts, cut into ½-in (1.3-cm) strips (approximately 114 yd [104 m] of strips)

Warping and Weaving

Sett: 12 EPI

Weave structure: Plain weave

Width in reed: 9 in (23 cm)

Wind a 3-yd (2.75-m) warp of 108 ends and warp your loom by your desired method. Set up the loom for plain weave. After allowing at least 8 in (20 cm) of warp yarn for fringe, weave a header of at least an inch with waste yarn to spread the warp and provide an anchor for adding floating selvedges and a place to secure a temple. If desired, begin with leaving a 27-in (70-cm) weft yarn tail for hemstitching.

Under high tension, weave in plain weave, beginning with six picks of weft yarn only and then alternating one pick of weft rag with two picks of weft yarn. Weave for 65 in (170 cm) or to the desired length, finishing with six picks of weft yarn, and hemstitching, if desired. Secure with 1 in (2.5 cm) of waste yarn, and cut from loom, allowing at least 8 in (20 cm) for fringe.

Finishing

Finished dimensions: 7½ in (19 cm) x 57 in (145 cm), excluding fringe

Finish fringe as desired. Twisting or braiding is recommended to keep the fine yarns from tangling and fraying in washing and wearing the scarf.

Follow wet-finishing instructions for **bamboo warp/silk rag** on page 27. Machine-dry with a large towel on low or no heat, checking every 20 minutes, until dry. Using an iron set on low to medium, hard press with steam, using iron to square up corners and straighten ends.

Care

Hand wash in cold water with mild detergent or shampoo. Rinse well and spin water out in washing machine set on spin or in a salad spinner. Dry and press as for **Finishing**.

Bright Bamboo Scarf

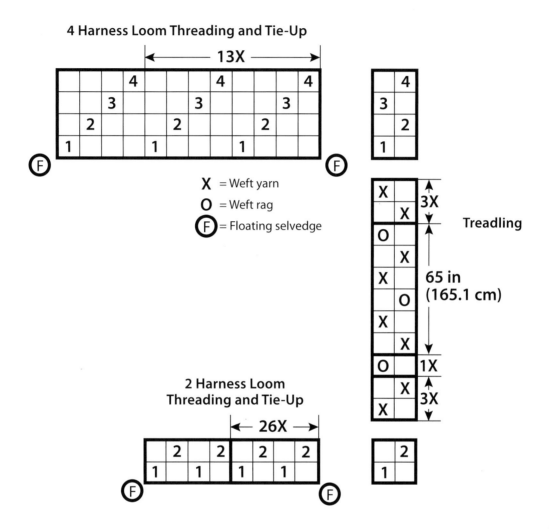

4 Harness Loom Threading and Tie-Up

X = Weft yarn
O = Weft rag
F = Floating selvedge

Treadling

65 in
(165.1 cm)

2 Harness Loom
Threading and Tie-Up

Recycled Silk Strip Yarn Scarf

W hile I truly enjoy the process of finding and preparing rags to use in weaving, I understand and sympathize with those without the time or patience for it, or who simply don't find that part of rag weaving enjoyable.

Luckily, there are commercial yarns now that are made from strips of recycled silk garments sewn or knotted together. Many of these are made of sari silk or other traditional clothing by companies that focus on employing women and paying living wages.

In terms of quality, these yarns are hit or miss. Check each skein to see whether the silk feels soft and whether you like the colors. The strips are usually cut quite a bit wider than I prefer, so the resulting fabric will be heavier and coarser than the other scarves in this book. However, using these yarns is a great way to recycle if you don't enjoy the creative destruction process as much as I do!

Materials

Warp: 8/2 tencel (3,360 yd/lb), Valley Yarns, Shale, 342 yd (312.75 m), and Black, 96 yd (87.75 m)

Weft yarn: Black tencel, 228 yd (208 m)

Weft rags: Silk Chiffon Ribbon Yarn (227 yd/lb), Himalaya Yarn, Multicolor, 50 yd (45.75 m)

Warping and Weaving

Sett: 16 EPI

Weave structure: Plain weave

Width in reed: 8³/₄ in (22.2 cm)

Wind a 3-yd warp of 114 ends Slate and 32 ends Black. Warp your loom by your desired method, following the chart given for the stripe pattern. Set up the loom for plain weave. After allowing at least 8 in (20 cm) of warp yarn for fringe, weave a header of at least an inch with waste yarn to spread the warp and provide an anchor for adding floating selvedges and a place to secure a temple. If desired, begin with leaving a 26-in (66-cm) weft yarn tail for hemstitching.

Under high tension, weave in plain weave, beginning with six picks of weft yarn only and then alternating one pick of weft rag with two picks of weft yarn. Weave the entire 50-yd (45.75-m) skein, or to desired length, finishing with six picks of weft yarn, and hemstitching, if desired. Secure with 1 in (2.5 cm) of waste yarn, and cut from loom, allowing at least 8 in (20 cm) for fringe.

Finishing

Finished dimensions: 7¹/₂ in (19 cm) x 51 in (130 cm), excluding fringe

Finish fringe as desired. Twisting or braiding is recommended to keep the fine yarns from tangling and fraying in washing and wearing the scarf.

Follow wet-finishing instructions for **tencel warp/silk rag** on page 27. Machine-dry with a large towel on low or no heat, checking every 20 minutes, until dry. Using an iron set on low to medium, hard press with steam, using iron to square up corners and straighten ends.

Care

Hand wash in cold water with mild detergent or shampoo. Rinse well and spin water out in washing machine set on spin or in a salad spinner. Dry and press as for **Finishing**.

Recycled silk ribbon yarn made by a women's cooperative.

AMANDA ROBINETTE

AMANDA ROBINETTE

This yarn consisted of strips of silk about 1 in (2.5 cm) wide knotted together end-to-end. Because I didn't want knots in my weaving, I cut apart the strips at each knot and wove those colors in the order they were presented in the skein. You could, of course, choose to leave the knots in if you would like something more rustic-looking, or you could sort the strips by color and design your own striping pattern.

Recycled Silk Strip Yarn Scarf

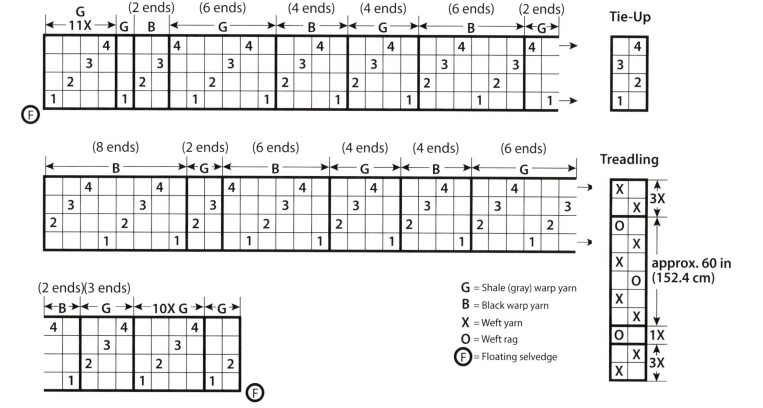

G = Shale (gray) warp yarn
B = Black warp yarn
X = Weft yarn
O = Weft rag
Ⓕ = Floating selvedge

Elongated Twill Scarf

Sakiori was made in plain weave, for the most part. The household looms of rural Japan were two-harness looms, and the women doing the weaving were pressed for time to make their family's textiles.

Many weavers today, though, have a minimum of four shafts on their looms, so why should we limit ourselves to plain weave?

This scarf uses a twill pattern from *Orimono Soshiki Hen* (Yoshida, Kiju, Japan, 1903: p. 220, Figure 1), an old Japanese weaving textbook. It is a simple twill that can undoubtedly be found as well in weaving books from Germany, England, and other places. The pattern results in strong diagonal lines and the fabric takes on a stitched or quilted appearance.

I used a variegated tencel in the warp and weft that has shades of blue and gold. The silk rag came from a friend's black-and-white patterned silk brocade dress. This is a good place to note the difference between weaving with plain weave silk rags and those with a brocade or other complex weave structure. Because plain weave results in a perpendicular array, shedding is kept to a minimum. Once the cut or torn edge has shedded back to one of the long warp or weft threads, it pretty much stops. With a complex weave structure, you are cutting across threads that don't run parallel to your cut, and the result tends to be thready. When it comes to rag weaving, this can be considered a design element rather than a detriment. If it doesn't suit your taste, though, you might consider sticking with plain weave fabrics.

Materials

Warp: 8/2 tencel (3,360 yd/lb), Valley Yarns, Mountain
  Stream Combo, 324 yd (296 m)
Weft yarn: Same as warp yarn, 150 yd (137 m)
Weft rags: Silk brocade from ladies' dress, cut into
  ½-in (1.3-cm) strips (approximately 67 yd [61 m]
  of strips)

Warping and Weaving

Sett: 24 EPI
Weave structure: Twill (see chart)
Width in reed: 6 in (15.25 cm)

Wind a 2¼-yd (2-m) warp of 144 ends and warp your
loom by your desired method. Set up the loom for twill
pattern as charted. After allowing at least 8 in (20 cm)
of warp yarn for fringe, weave a header of at least an
inch (2.5 cm) with waste yarn to spread the warp and
provide an anchor for adding floating selvedges and a
place to secure a temple. If desired, begin with leaving
an 18-in (45.75-cm) weft yarn tail for hemstitching.

Here you can see the black and white pattern on the dress fabric, and what it looks like after weaving. As you
can see, I sampled the fabric with my warp yarn to make sure I liked the result before weaving my scarf.

Under high tension, weave six picks of weft yarn only in plain weave and then begin pattern. Alternate one pick of weft rag in twill pattern with one pick of weft yarn in plain weave. Weave for 50 in (130 cm) or to the desired length, finishing with six picks of weft yarn, and hemstitching, if desired. Secure with 1 in (2.5 cm) of waste yarn, and cut from loom, allowing at least 8 in (20 cm) for fringe.

Finishing

Finished dimensions: 5 in (12.7 cm) x 42 in (107 cm), excluding fringe

Finish fringe as desired, removing waste yarn. Twisting or braiding is recommended to keep the fine yarns from tangling and fraying in washing and wearing the scarf.

Follow wet-finishing instructions for **tencel warp/silk rag** on page 27. Machine-dry with a large towel on low or no heat, checking every 20 minutes, until dry. Using an iron set on low to medium, hard press with steam, using iron to square up corners and straighten ends.

Care

Hand wash in cold water with mild detergent or shampoo. Rinse well and spin water out in washing machine set on spin or in a salad spinner. Dry and press as for **Finishing**.

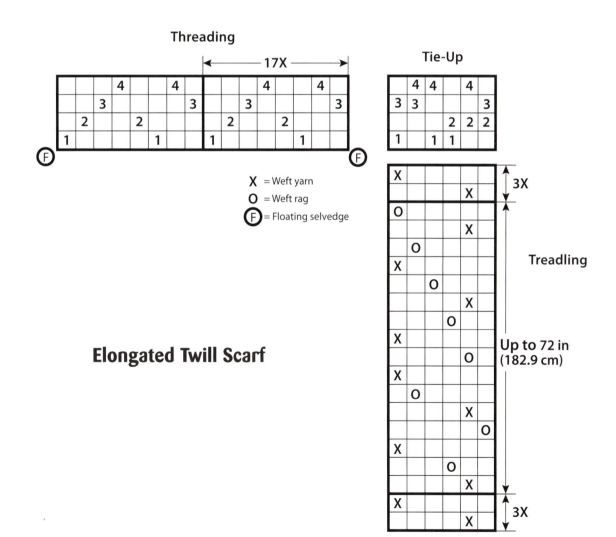

Threading

17X

X = Weft yarn
O = Weft rag
F = Floating selvedge

Tie-Up

Treadling

3X

Up to 72 in (182.9 cm)

3X

Elongated Twill Scarf

Bamboo Overshot Scarf

Overshot is a uniquely European and North American tradition. Most people have seen overshot coverlets in colonial reproduction movies or at living history sites. It was a popular weave structure at the time because it was a way to get a more complex pattern out of the four-harness looms that people usually had in their homes. Among the Japanese rural communities, with their two-harness looms, overshot was not historically used.

In overshot, a heavier pattern weft is alternated with a lighter weft yarn woven in plain weave. By alternating a pattern weft with a plain weave weft, long vertical (warp-wise) floats are prevented and the fabric remains stable. It is ideal for sakiori, because the rag strips can easily serve as the heavier pattern weft, and alternating with a weft yarn in plain weave is something we are already doing. The horizontal floats that occur in overshot patterns are an accent that shows off a pretty rag, and they double as a place you can point to if you need to prove to someone that your beautiful new scarf is made from rags!

Materials

Warp: Bambu 7 (2,100 yd/lb), Silk City Fibers, Onyx 360, 300 yd (274 m)

Weft yarn: Same as warp yarn, 123 yd (112.5 m)

Weft rags: Lightweight silk from shirt and shorts, cut or torn into ½-in (1.3-cm) strips (approximately 62 yd [56.7 m] of strips)

Warping and Weaving

Sett: 12 EPI

Weave structure: Plain weave

Width in reed: 8.2 in (20.8 cm)

Wind a 3-yd (2.75 m) warp of 98 ends and warp your loom by your desired method, following the chart given for the overshot pattern. After allowing at least 8 in (20 cm) of warp yarn for fringe, weave a header of at least an inch with waste yarn to spread the warp and provide an anchor for adding floating selvedges and a place to secure a temple. If desired, begin with leaving a 25-in (63.5-cm) weft yarn tail for hemstitching.

Under high tension, weave in plain weave, beginning with six picks of weft yarn only and then alternating one pick of weft rag with two picks of weft yarn. After nine picks of rag, weave two picks in weft yarn. Begin overshot pattern, alternating each pick of weft rag with one pick of weft yarn, as indicated in chart. After last pick of weft rag in overshot pattern, resume plain weave pattern by weaving two picks of weft yarn, one pick of weft rag, and so on. Weave to 3 in (7.6 cm) short of the desired length and then repeat the overshot chart. Finish by resuming plain weave pattern for nine more picks of weft rag, then six picks of weft yarn, and hemstitching, if desired. Secure with 1 in (2.5 cm) of waste yarn, and cut from loom, allowing at least 8 in (20 cm) for fringe.

Finishing

Finished dimensions: 7 in (17.75 cm) x 45 in (114.3 cm) excluding fringe

Finish fringe as desired. Twisting or braiding is recommended to keep the fine yarns from tangling and fraying in washing and wearing the scarf.

Follow wet-finishing instructions for **bamboo warp/silk rag** on page 27. Machine-dry with a large towel on low or no heat, checking every 20 minutes, until dry. Using an iron set on low to medium, hard press with steam, using iron to square up corners and straighten ends.

Care

Hand wash in cold water with mild detergent or shampoo. Rinse well and spin water out in washing machine set on spin or in a salad spinner. Dry and press as for **Finishing**.

Bamboo Overshot Scarf

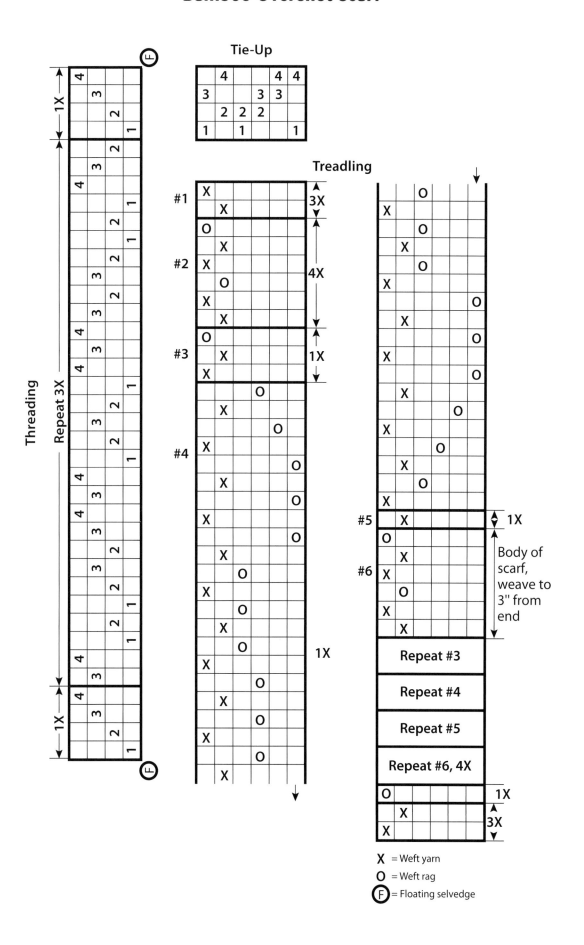

X = Weft yarn

O = Weft rag

F = Floating selvedge

Dogwood Flower Overshot Scarf with Tencel

This is another scarf with an overshot border, this time with a tencel warp and weft yarn. I also used a contrasting weft rag to make the flowers stand out more.

This pattern reminds me of dogwood flowers, with their orderly, four-petaled blooms. Their bright white or pink colors always stand out against the drab, early spring background.

Materials

Warp: 8/2 tencel (3,360 yd/lb), Valley Yarns, Painted Desert Combo, 441 yd (403.25 m)
Weft yarn: Same as warp yarn, 315 yd (288 m)
Weft rags: Lightweight silk from four women's blouses plus a small amount of contrast color rag for the pattern, cut into ½-in (1.3-cm) strips (approximately 158 yd [144.5 m] of strips)

Warping and Weaving

Sett: 16 EPI
Weave structure: Plain weave plus overshot
Width in reed: 9.2 in (23.4 cm)

Wind a 3-yd (2.75-m) warp of 147 ends and warp your loom by your desired method, following the chart as indicated for the overshot pattern. After allowing at least 8 in (20 cm) of warp yarn for fringe, weave a header of at least an inch with waste yarn to spread the warp and provide an anchor for adding floating selvedges and a place to secure a temple. If desired, begin with leaving a 28-in (71-cm) weft yarn tail for hemstitching.

Under high tension, weave in plain weave, beginning with six picks of weft yarn only and then alternating one pick of weft rag with two picks of weft yarn. Weave for 3 in (7.6 cm), cutting weft rag and weaving in end. Switch to contrast weft rag and begin overshot pattern, weaving one pick weft rag in pattern alternating with one pick weft yarn in plain weave. Finish chart, cut pattern weft rag, and weave in end. Resume plain weave pattern with weft rag and weft yarn. Weave to 5 in (12.7 cm) short of the desired length and repeat the overshot pattern. Resume plain weave pattern for 3 in (7.6 cm), finishing with six picks of weft yarn, and hemstitching, if desired. Secure with 1 in (2.5 cm) of waste yarn, and cut from loom, allowing at least 8 in (20 cm) for fringe.

Finishing

Finished dimensions: 7½ in (19 cm) x 72 in (183 cm) excluding fringe

Finish fringe as desired. Twisting or braiding is recommended to keep the fine yarns from tangling and fraying in washing and wearing the scarf.

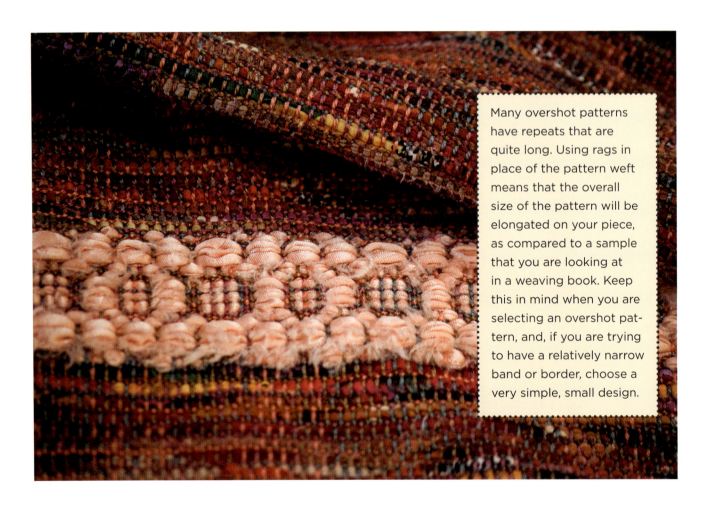

Many overshot patterns have repeats that are quite long. Using rags in place of the pattern weft means that the overall size of the pattern will be elongated on your piece, as compared to a sample that you are looking at in a weaving book. Keep this in mind when you are selecting an overshot pattern, and, if you are trying to have a relatively narrow band or border, choose a very simple, small design.

Follow wet-finishing instructions for **tencel warp/silk rag** on page 27. Machine-dry with a large towel on low or no heat, checking every 20 minutes, until dry. Using an iron set on low to medium, hard press with steam, using iron to square up corners and straighten ends.

Care

Hand wash in cold water with mild detergent or shampoo. Rinse well and spin water out in washing machine set on spin or in a salad spinner. Dry and press as for **Finishing**.

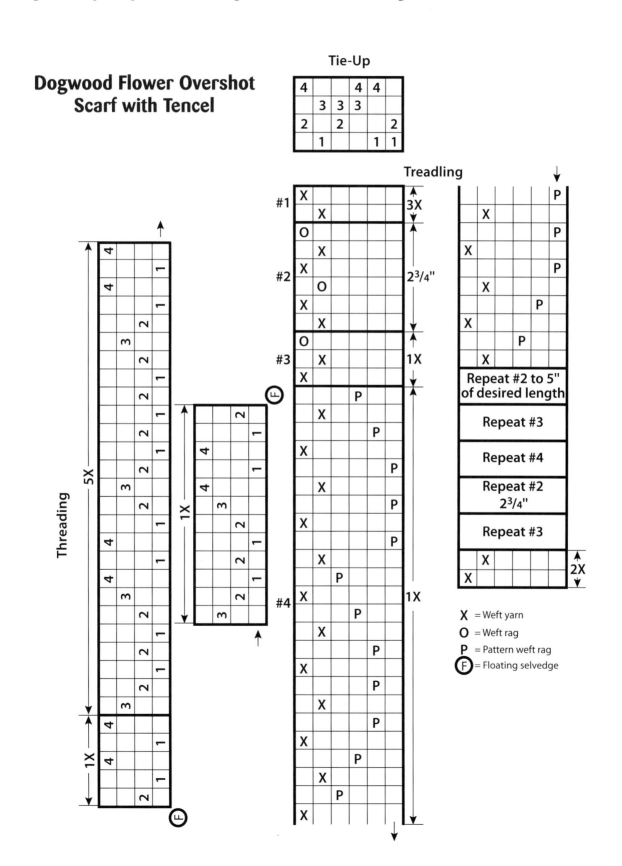

Dogwood Flower Overshot Scarf with Tencel

Tie-Up

Treadling

Threading

X = Weft yarn
O = Weft rag
P = Pattern weft rag
Ⓕ = Floating selvedge

Making Memories

Cloth holds memories for all of us, even more so for those of us who make it. Our affinity for cloth makes us pay more attention to color, texture, and structure than most people. Links exist between textiles and the memories made around them. We remember the fabric of the little dresses and shirts of our babies, of the shirt we wore on our favorite vacation, of the outfit we picked out for a special moment in our lives. Seeing these fabrics again calls up vivid memories.

Unfortunately, cloth doesn't survive the ravages of time as well as those memories. We may save a treasured textile, only to unpack it years later and see that it is falling apart, has yellowed, or pests have been at it. But don't despair—you are a weaver, and you can save that cloth, put it to good use, and preserve its link to your memories.

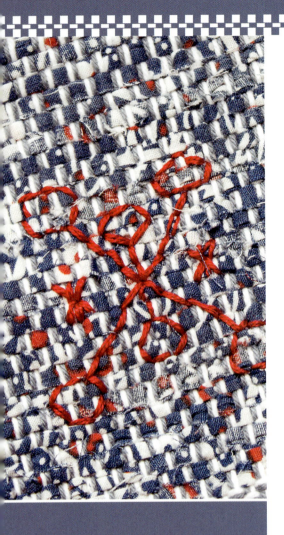

Mom's Housecoat Mug Rugs

A few years ago, near Christmas, a good friend's mom lost her fight with cancer. As I helped my friend go through her mom's things, I asked if she and other members of the family would like to have some woven items made from some of her clothes as one way to preserve her memory and feel her presence in their lives.

I came away with a bag of old clothes and a few ideas. Among the clothes, the item I loved the most was a fabulous old cotton housecoat with a retro blue and red pattern. I knew that I wanted to make some vintage-y mug rugs from it to give to the family.

Mug rugs are basically just miniature rag rugs to be used as coasters. (They also make nice dollhouse rugs.) I like to make mug rugs on smaller looms, such as my Peacock two-harness 12-inch children's loom (The Handcrafters, Waupun, Wisconsin) or a rigid heddle loom. I find it can be a bit unwieldy to make such a small project on a big floor loom, and the narrow warp and rag strip width make it a lot easier to get a firm beat on the rags even without the weight of a floor loom's beater bar.

A 2-yd (1.8-m) warp will easily yield eight or more mug rugs, depending on loom waste, and they are a quick and easy gift to make. I chose to add some simple red embroidery to add to the vintage blue-and-red color scheme.

The Peacock loom.

A beautifully retro housecoat.

I made these mug rugs on a rigid heddle loom like this one. Usually when I make mug rugs I sett them at 12 EPI, but carpet warp is too heavy to fit through the holes in a 12-dent rigid heddle (one of the hazards of rigid heddle weaving!). Luckily, mug rugs are not very exacting. I thought 8 EPI might be a bit too unstructured, so I opted to put two ends in each slot and hole of an 8-dent rigid heddle for a total of 16 EPI.

Materials

Warp: 8/4 carpet warp (1,600 yd/lb), Maysville, Slate Gray and White, 72 yd (65.8 m) each plus extra for headers

Weft rags: Cotton housecoat, cut into ¹/₂-in (1.3-cm) strips (one housecoat will yield many, many mug rugs, if desired)

Special equipment: Supplemental beater or weaving sword, thin cardboard cut into 1-in (2.5-cm) x 6-in (15.25-cm) strips

Warping and Weaving

Sett: 16 EPI (2 ends per slot/hole in an 8-dent rigid heddle)

Weave structure: Plain weave

Width in reed: 4.5 in (11.5 cm)

Wind a 2-yd (1.8-m) warp of 36 ends of each color and warp your loom by your desired method, placing one end of each color together in each slot and hole (or heddle, if using a harness loom). Set up the loom for plain weave. Weave a header of waste yarn to spread the warp.

Under high tension, weave in plain weave, beginning with six picks of doubled warp yarn only and then

Place the cardboard strips between the mug rugs to act as spacers for the fringe.

switching to weft rag only. Weave each mug rug so that the rag-woven portion is 4 in (10 cm), finishing with six picks of doubled warp yarn.

Open the next shed and place a cardboard strip against the end of the mug rug. Change the shed and

place another strip. Begin weaving the next mug rug as above.

After weaving the last mug rug, secure with waste yarn and cut from loom.

Finishing

Finished dimensions: 3¾ in (9.5 cm) x 4¾ in (12 cm), excluding fringe

Using a sewing machine, stitch straight across the beginning and end of each mug rug right at the edge of the header (between the cardboard or the waste yarn and the header). Go back and zigzag stitch in the same area, being careful to get all the way to the selvedges.

Using scissors or a rotary cutter, cut between each pair of cardboard strips and remove the cardboard. Carefully remove waste yarn from first and last mug rugs, and trim fringes to desired length.

Cut the mug rugs apart between the cardboard spacers.

An easy way to neatly cut your fringes to the same length is to use a rotary cutter and a guide.

It is unnecessary to wet-finish mug rugs, since it is desirable for them to be structured instead of soft, and the rags were cleaned before weaving.

Care

Hand wash in cold water with mild detergent. Rinse well, press out excess water with a towel, and lay flat to dry (a cooling rack from the kitchen works for this).

Mom's Housecoat Mug Rugs

Threading

← 9X →

	2		2
1		1	

Tie-Up

	2
1	

X = Double warp yarn
O = Weft rag

Treadling

X		¼ in (.6 cm)
	X	
O		4 in (10.2 cm)
	O	
X		¼ in (.6 cm)
	X	

Walking on Sunshine T-shirt Rug

You are my sunshine
My only sunshine
You make me happy
When skies are gray

—*Jimmie Davis*
and Charles Mitchell,
"You Are My Sunshine"

Pretty in pink!

AMANDA ROBINETTE

I had a lot of fun dressing my daughter when she was little. Let's face it—little girls' clothing is cuter than that of little boys. There are so many pretty prints and outfits for sale, and my mother enjoyed making adorable little dresses and playsuits for her as well. I was certainly disappointed when I shopped for my son and discovered that most little boys' clothes are basic T-shirts and bottoms with maybe an embroidered truck, baseball, or dinosaur on them.

My mother also made a lot of my maternity clothes, especially for my first pregnancy with my daughter. Most of those were still in great shape and I was able to pass them on to other expectant mothers, but some had become worn out or stained. The same was true of my daughter's baby clothes (although I kept some of the really special outfits for future babies in the family instead of giving them away).

I used some of the castoff clothes in rag rugs, but a lot of the clothes were made of knitted, rather than woven, fabric. Knitwear (such as T-shirts) tends to cause irregular selvedges because it is stretchy and each item has different draw-in. Some years ago I came up with my own way of solving this problem, by cutting loops from shirts, pants, and dresses. (See pages 68 and 69 for more on making T-shirt yarn.) By stretching the loops until they lose their elasticity, they become stable weft material. The loops can then be joined using a loop-to-loop connection: Place the end of one loop (A) over the other one (B). Pull the end of loop A down through the end of

loop B, and pull tight. I like to cut all my loops and then sit among the piles of loops and make a giant basketball-sized ball of yarn for a rug, but if you prefer you can loop as you go while sitting at the loom. The loops should be cut about ½ in (1.3 cm) thick, as they will thin when stretched out and then be doubled in the shed.

After I learned how to use knitwear as rug weft, I made a very special rug from my daughter's and my old clothes. I call it *Walking on Sunshine* because "You Are My Sunshine" was the special song I would sing for my little girl. This rug is made from my memories of my long sunshiny days with my July baby.

Materials

Warp: 8/4 carpet warp (1,600 yd/lb), Maysville, 833 yd (762 m) in desired colors plus extra for headers; warp stripe design pictured is by the author

> Carpet warp comes in a lot of colors, and so do rags! Find your own favorite color or striping pattern to enhance your rag colors.

Weft rags: Tubular knitwear, cut into ½-in (1.3-cm) loops and joined together, about a basketball-sized ball of yarn, or about 160 yd (146 m)

Walking on Sunshine T-shirt Rug

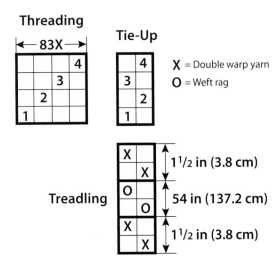

Warping and Weaving

Sett: 12 EPI
Weave structure: Plain weave
Width in reed: 27²/₃ in (70.2 cm)

Wind a 2½-yd (2.3-m) warp of 332 ends and warp your loom by your desired method. Set up the loom for plain weave. Weave a header of waste yarn to spread the warp, allowing length for fringe, if desired.

Under high tension, weave in plain weave, beginning with 1½ in (3.8 cm) of doubled warp yarn only for a rolled hem, or, if you prefer fringe, weave ½ in (1.3 cm) for a header. Next, weave with the weft rag only until rug measures 54 in (137 cm) or desired length. Switch to doubled warp yarn and weave hem or header as before. Weave at least 1 in (2.5 cm) of waste yarn to secure ends and cut from loom, allowing length for fringe, if desired.

Finishing

Finished dimensions: 27 in (68.5 cm) x 48 in (123 cm)

For rolled hem, using a sewing machine, zigzag stitch across the beginning and end of rug right at the edge of the header (between the waste yarn and the header). Using scissors, cut away waste yarn from beginning and end, being careful not to cut the sewing lines just made. Roll hem and hand-sew.

For fringe, remove waste yarn and knot fringe against header. Trim ends even.

It is unnecessary to wet-finish rag rugs, since it is desirable for them to be structured instead of soft, and the rags were cleaned before weaving.

Care

Machine-wash in cold water with mild detergent. Hang to dry. Do not machine-dry—this will cause the carpet warp header to shrink and pucker the ends of the rug.

The loop-to-loop method creates small knots that make the rug a little bumpy. If you don't like that, you can spiral-cut circular knitwear in a continuous 1-in (2.5-cm) strip, pulling it tight as you go. There are a lot of online tutorials and videos for making T-shirt yarn, or "tarn," and different people have come up with different methods. I encourage you to try these out and find your favorite way of preparing knitwear for use as weft.

Knots form bumps on rugs made using the loop-to-loop method.

A smooth surface results from using a spiral-cut, continuous strip.

Cut Loops to Make T-shirt Yarn

1 Cut loops ½ in (1.3 cm) wide.

2 Overlap the loop ends.

3 Pull the top loop down through the bottom loop.

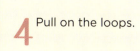

4 Pull on the loops.

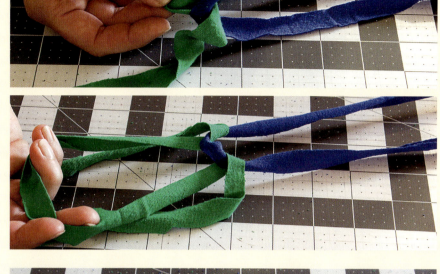

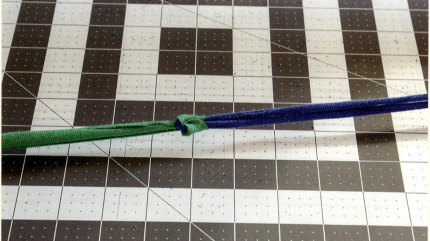

5 Pull the knot and the entire length of both loops tight to stretch out the fabric and minimize its elasticity.

6 The final result.

Cozy Flannel Baby Blanket

A warm cotton flannel shirt feels just right on a cold winter's day, and there is nothing cozier than a flannel nightgown or pajamas when there is a chill in the air. You can pass some of that comfort along by turning your old shirts and pajamas into a soft baby blanket for a new little one to enjoy.

Materials

Warp: Laceweight 100% Pure Soysilk (6,370 yd/lb), Stranded in Oz hand-dyed, Antarctica II, 2 skeins

Weft yarn: 8/2 unmercerized cotton (3,360 yd/lb), Valley Yarns, Dark Teal, 650 yd (595 m)

Weft rags: Cotton flannel from shirts and pajamas, cut into ¼-in (.6-cm) strips (approximately 264 yd [241 m] of strips)

Warping and Weaving

Sett: 16 EPI
Weave structure: Plain weave
Width in reed: 38 in (97 cm)

Wind a 2¼-yd (2-m) warp of 608 ends and warp your loom by your desired method. Set up the loom for plain weave. Weave a header of at least an inch with waste yarn to spread the warp and provide an anchor for adding floating selvedges and a place to secure a temple.

Under high tension, weave in plain weave, beginning with 1½ in (3.8 cm) of weft yarn only for the rolled hem. Next, weave one pick of weft rag alternating with two picks of weft yarn. After weaving 48 in (122 cm) or to desired length, repeat hem. Weave at least 1 in (2.5 cm) of waste yarn to secure ends and cut from loom.

Finishing

Finished dimensions: 36 in (91 cm) x 44 in (111.75 cm)

Using a sewing machine, stitch straight across the beginning and end of baby blanket right at the edge of the hem (between the waste yarn and the hem). Go back and zigzag stitch in the same area, being careful to get all the way to the selvedges.

Using scissors, cut away waste yarn from beginning and end, being careful not to cut the sewing lines just made.

Follow wet-finishing instructions for **azlon (soysilk) warp/cotton rag** on page 27. Hang to dry; tumble briefly in dryer with large towel on low or no heat to soften. Using an iron set on low to medium, hard press with steam, using iron to square up corners and straighten ends. Roll hem and hand-sew.

Care

Machine-wash on delicate or hand wash in cold water with mild detergent. Hang to dry; tumble briefly in dryer to soften.

AMANDA ROBINETTE

For this blanket, I used a soysilk warp. Soysilk is made from the waste products remaining after soy is processed into food products. Technically, it is a regenerated protein fiber called azlon, a family that also includes yarns made from milk and corn. In the skein, this yarn has a springy, lightweight feel, similar to cotton.

4 Harness Loom Threading and Tie-Up

Repeat 150X

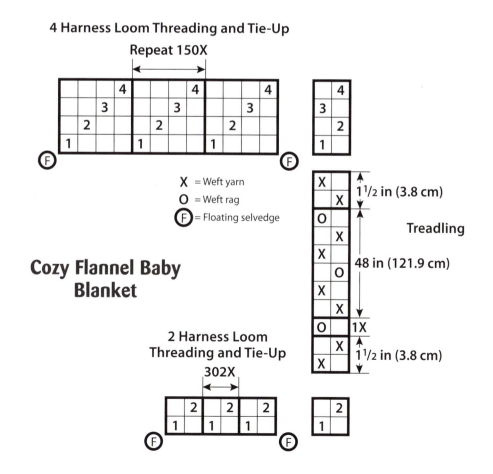

X = Weft yarn
O = Weft rag
F = Floating selvedge

Cozy Flannel Baby Blanket

Treadling

1½ in (3.8 cm)

48 in (121.9 cm)

1X

1½ in (3.8 cm)

2 Harness Loom Threading and Tie-Up

302X

Colors of the Caribbean Baby Blanket

When I was in college, I had the wonderful experience of taking a one-month summer course that took place entirely on Caribbean islands. During a two-week stay on Barbados, some of us went to Saint Lucia for the weekend (it was a rough life, but someone had to do it). There, some friends and I visited a marketplace that was set up for the cruise-ship traffic, and I bought a vast, colorful cotton gauze skirt. It fastened with a drawstring but had so much fabric it could have fit around the four of us, easily. I loved the colors (purple and blue with orange and pink flowers) and the print, and I loved wearing flowing cotton skirts, but this was just too much. Twenty-five years later, it was still in my closet and had almost never been worn.

I wanted to make something with it, and thought that the gauze might prove thin enough to make a lightweight baby blanket. I found a similar skirt in bright orange, green, and blue stripes at the thrift shop. When I had the two skirts side by side and noted the dominant blue and orange colors, it occurred to me that they reminded me of something.

(Continued on page 77)

My original skirt, right, and a thrifted version, left.

(Continued from page 74)

My son was six years old when he told me he wanted to learn how to weave. Other weaving parents can relate to the heart-in-the-mouth moment that this causes. We want our offspring to love weaving as much as we do, but we know that we must tread lightly, because to push the issue is to push them away. So, very casually, and expecting him to lose interest at any moment, I began the process. "What do you want to make? What colors? How do you want to arrange them?" When he remained interested throughout this beginning (answers: "A scarf for me, blue and orange, warp stripes"), I hopefully set about warping my 12-inch Peacock student loom. He was very decisive about the warp design. It was to be 1 in (2.5 cm) blue and orange stripes, but it should start with blue and end with orange—no symmetry for this little guy.

I watched in mild surprise as he sat on the floor in my studio, next to me as I wove on a floor loom, and over the course of a few days wove an entirely respectable length of scarf. He had nearly perfect selvedges and almost never needed help from me, except when it came to starting a new shuttle of yarn.

He still wears his scarf proudly, and, although he has not shown the slightest interest in weaving anything else yet, I hold out hope for the future. I designed this baby blanket with blue and orange stripes in honor of his early weaving achievement (although I preferred to begin and end with the same color stripes). Subtle warp stripes in hand-dyed tencel give the finished blanket a slight gingham look. The end result is a very lightweight blanket suitable for spring and summer babies. The size given is for newborns or for use as a blanket for a car seat or stroller; to make it larger, increase the width and length of the warp accordingly.

AMANDA ROBINETTE

Diligently weaving on the Peacock loom.

The same boy still loves to wear his scarf many years later.

Materials

Warp: Laceweight tencel (2,520 yd/lb), Prism Delicato Layers, Peony, 384 yd (351 m), and Jasper, 408 yd (373 m)

Weft yarn: 10/2 perle cotton (4,200 yd/lb), Valley Yarns, Daffodil, 264 yd (241.4 m); 20/2 perle cotton (8,400 yd/lb), Purple, 205 yd (187.4 m); Laceweight tencel (2,520 yd/lb), Prism Delicato Layers, Jasper, small amount for hems

Weft rags: Cotton gauze from two full skirts, cut into ¼-in (.6-cm) strips (approximately 132 yd [121 m] of orange strips and 140 yd [128 m] of blue strips)

Warping and Weaving

Sett: 12 EPI

Weave structure: Plain weave

Width in reed: 33 in (84 cm)

Wind a 2-yd (1.8-m) warp of 204 ends Jasper and 192 ends Peony and warp your loom by your desired method, following the warp stripe pattern given. Set up the loom for plain weave. Weave a header of at least an inch with waste yarn to spread the warp and provide an anchor for adding floating selvedges and a place to secure a temple.

Under high tension, weave in plain weave, beginning with 1 in (2.5 cm) of Jasper tencel only for the rolled hem. Next, weave one pick of weft rag alternating with two picks of weft yarn. Begin and end the first stripe with Daffodil perle cotton and alternate with orange rag until there are eight picks of rag weft. After the last two picks of Daffodil, switch to the blue/purple rag alternating with the Purple perle cotton. Each stripe going forward consists of eight picks of rag weft, each followed by two picks of the corresponding perle cotton. After weaving 36 in (91 cm) or to desired length, and ending with an orange stripe, repeat hem. Weave at least 1 in (2.5 cm) of waste yarn to secure ends and cut from loom.

Finishing

Finished dimensions: 28½ in (72.4 cm) x 32¼ in (82 cm)

Using a sewing machine, stitch straight across the beginning and end of baby blanket right at the edge of the hem (between the waste yarn and the hem). Go back and zigzag stitch in the same area, being careful to get all the way to the selvedges.

Using scissors, cut away waste yarn from beginning and end, being careful not to cut the sewing lines just made.

Follow wet-finishing instructions for **tencel warp/ cotton rag** on page 27. Hang to dry; tumble briefly with large towel on low or no heat in dryer to soften. Using an iron set on low to medium, hard press with steam, using iron to square up corners and straighten ends. Roll hem and hand-sew.

Care

Machine-wash on delicate or hand-wash in cold water with mild detergent. Hang to dry; tumble briefly in dryer to soften.

AMANDA ROBINETTE

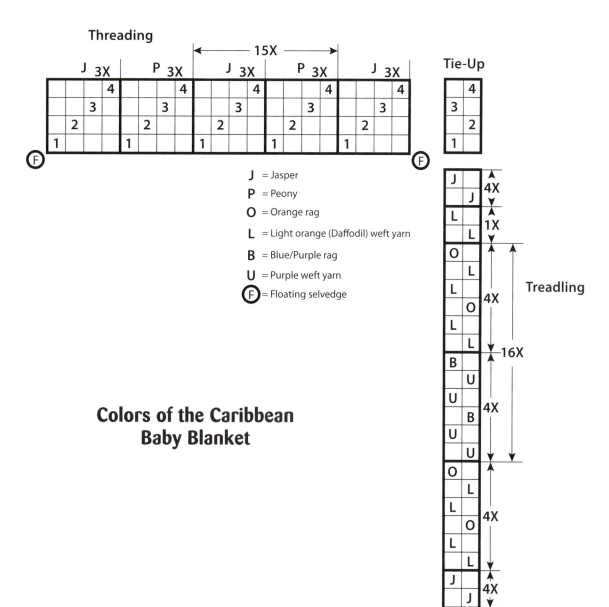

Threading

J = Jasper
P = Peony
O = Orange rag
L = Light orange (Daffodil) weft yarn
B = Blue/Purple rag
U = Purple weft yarn
Ⓕ = Floating selvedge

**Colors of the Caribbean
Baby Blanket**

Tie-Up

Treadling

Wedding Dress Bed Runner

There is a lot of emotion woven into the fabric of a wedding gown. It is chosen with great care by the bride, who may have been imagining the perfect dress since childhood. It is imbued with hope for the future, optimism, and love. After the wedding, many dresses are carefully packed away "for someday," when perhaps a daughter or granddaughter might like to wear it to her own wedding, making a tradition out of one person's choice.

Unfortunately, in most cases, that "someday" doesn't seem likely to arrive. Styles change, fabric deteriorates in basements and attics, and new brides want to make their own choices. After all, most of the brides packing away their dresses are not re-packing their mother's gown, but rather a new one they purchased. Today's brides seem less and less inclined to have the sort of wedding that requires anything fancier than a cocktail dress, and the puffy, lacy sleeves of the late 20th century have given way to unembellished, sleeveless sheaths.

So, what's a formerly blushing bride to do with that old dress that no one wants to wear or even re-fashion? It holds far too much significance to discard, but it only takes up space in that box in the attic. If only there was a way to have it out on display where she could see it and enjoy it. . . .

I wanted to make this project, but I wasn't quite ready to cut up my own wedding gown (yes, it is taking up space in a big box in the upstairs closet—puffy sleeves and all!). Fortunately for me, a friend of mine volunteered her gown for my use. It was an elaborate full gown with a long train and many lace embellishments, some of them beaded. The material seemed to be a very lightweight nylon, although there was no tag indicating the fabric content.

Bed runners have become popular design elements. They are usually 20–27 in (51–69 cm) wide and long enough to hang over the edges as they lay across the foot of the bed. Unlike other household textiles, they don't take a lot of abuse. They are not walked on or eaten near, and dripping cups are not rested on them. A bed runner is the perfect thing to make with the yards of white satin or silk in that special dress.

The photo to the right pictures the bride and her father on her wedding day. This dress and photo will always be special to my friend because she doesn't have many photos with her dad. I was so pleased to not only be making my vision a reality, but to be giving her another way to remember her father.

Materials

Warp: 8/2 Bamboo (3,360 yd/lb) Halcyon Yarn, White, 1,700 yd (1,154 m)
Weft yarn: Same as warp, 1,000 yd (914 m)
Weft rags: Wedding dress, cut into ½-in (1.3-cm) strips
Special equipment: Seam ripper, sharp pointy scissors

Warping and Weaving

Sett: 16 EPI
Weave structure: Overshot, Star of Bethlehem
Width in reed: 28.2 in (71.6 cm)

If the dress does not have a lot of material (full skirt, train, etc.), then you will need to make your runner narrower to get a good length out of it. Or, take some

Special notes: Wedding dresses come in all shapes, sizes, and fibers. In looking for a wedding dress to use in this project, I discovered that most thrift shop dresses are thin polyester or even a lightweight sort of plastic, similar to a tablecloth material but lighter. How you cut your strips is going to depend on the fabric with which you are working. If it is a thin polyester or nylon satin, then ½-in (1.3-cm) strips work well. If it is a heavier material, like the semi-plastics that I encountered, or if it is something like a raw silk, you will want to cut narrower strips. For the overshot pattern to look good, you want the rag to beat down to about two to three times the size of the weft yarn picks.

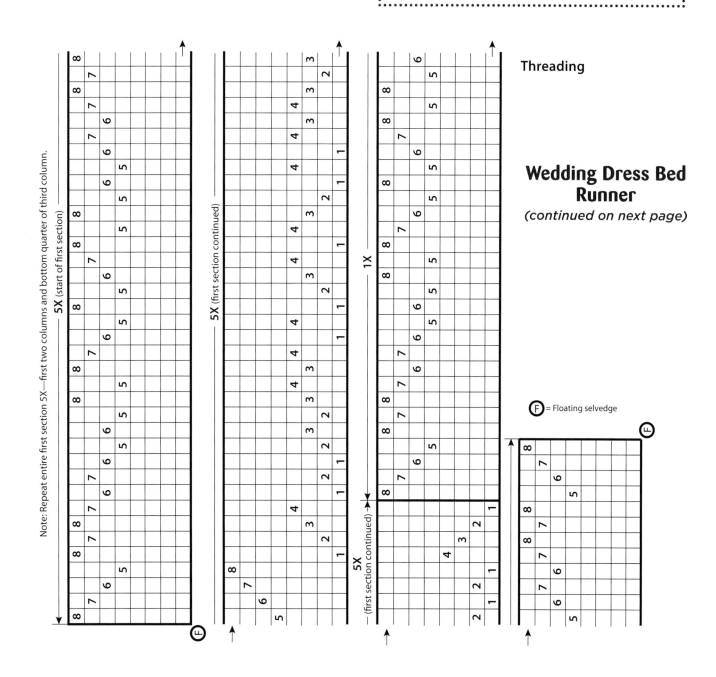

Threading

Wedding Dress Bed Runner
(continued on next page)

Ⓕ = Floating selvedge

(continued on next page)

Wedding Dress Bed Runner

(continued from previous page)

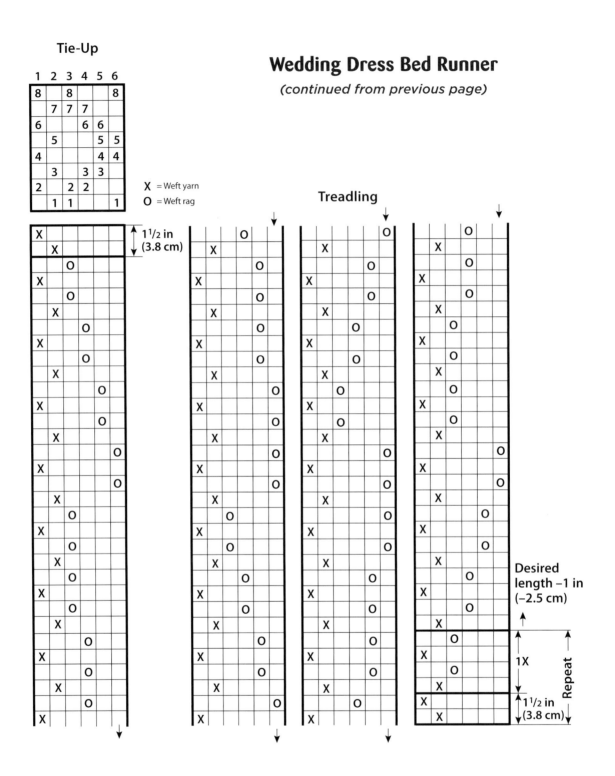

Tie-Up

Treadling

X = Weft yarn
O = Weft rag

1½ in (3.8 cm)

Desired length −1 in (−2.5 cm)

1X

Repeat

1½ in (3.8 cm)

samples with you to the thrift shop or fabric store and see if you can find anything close enough to mix together with the dress material. Just be sure to change every other rag pick between the two fabrics so there is no obvious dividing line.

Wedding dress construction tends to have a lot of support structures and linings, as well as surface embellishment. Separate the top layer of fabric from any linings or petticoats. Those are usually made from very different material that you won't want to mix with the fabric of the dress proper. If your dress has lace or bead elements or trims, I recommend carefully unpicking them as a unit (this may involve sacrificing some fabric by simply cutting around an element so that it will hold together). These can then be used as trim on the bed runner or to embellish a matching pillow or two, if desired.

Deconstruct the dress into sections free of rolled hems or other seams. You can make the weaving go faster by using the continuous strip method of cutting up these sections.

For a king-size bed runner, wind a 3¾-yd (3.4-m) warp of 451 ends and warp and tie-up your loom by your desired method, following the weaving chart given. Weave a header of at least an inch with waste yarn to spread the warp and provide an anchor for adding floating selvedges and a place to secure a temple.

Under high tension, weave a 1½-in (3.8-cm) header in plain weave with one strand of the weft yarn. Then switch to Star of Bethlehem treadling pattern, weaving one pick of weft rag in pattern alternating with one pick of weft yarn in tabby.

Weave until weft rag has been used up, to desired length, or until rag-woven portion measures 103 in (262 cm) for a king-sized bed runner. Next weave a 1½-in (3.8-cm) header as at the beginning. Weave waste yarn in plain weave to secure the piece.

Finishing

Finished dimensions: 26.5 in (67 cm) x 86 in (218 cm), excluding fringe

Using a sewing machine, stitch straight across the beginning and end of bed runner right at the edge of the header (between the waste yarn and the header). Go back and zigzag stitch in the same area, being careful to get all the way to the selvedges.

Using scissors, cut away waste yarn, being careful not to cut the sewing lines just made.

Hand wash with mild detergent if necessary, rinsing well and pressing out excess water by rolling bed runner in a towel. Lay flat to dry.

Sew a rolled hem on each end, being careful to turn it away from the right side of the weaving. If desired, hand-stitch decorative elements from the original dress onto the bed runner.

Care

This is one of those rare cases where dry cleaning is your best bet, especially if you have added some trim to the bed runner. When not in use, roll up with the right side on the inside.

If the dress you are using has a lot of lacy decorations, why not make a matching pillow for your new bed runner? Find some matching fabric and make the pillow cover in whatever size or shape you would like. Decide how to place the design elements and then, using a small running stitch, sew them onto the pillow top.

For the Home

One of the joys of weaving is to look around your home and see the products of your labor: the fingertip towel in the bathroom, the runner on the dining room table, the coverlet on the bed. . . .

In this section you will see some ideas for adding rag weaving to your home decor.

Under the Sea Desk Runner

I was inspired by the tropical sea colors of my daughter's room to make this desk runner. A glass top will keep the desk functional. Silk rag and hand-dyed tencel echo the colors of the walls and curtains, while a twill pattern adds depth both visually and in actual thickness of the cloth.

Materials

Warp: 10/2 tencel (4,200 yd/lb) Just Our Yarn hand-dyed, Almaza, 1,900 yd (1,737 m)

Weft yarn: Laceweight tencel (2,520 yd/lb), Prism Delicato Layers, 500 yd (457 m)

Weft rags: Lightweight silk garments, cut into ½-in (1.3-cm) strips, 275 yd (251 m)

Warping and Weaving

Sett: 28 EPI

Weave structure: Twill, see chart

Width in reed: 27¼ in (69 cm)

Wind a 2½-yd (2.3-m) warp of 760 ends. Warp your loom by your desired method, following the chart given for the twill pattern. Weave a header of at least an inch with waste yarn to spread the warp and provide an anchor for adding floating selvedges and a place to secure a temple.

Under high tension, weave in plain weave, beginning with 1 in (2.5 cm) of weft yarn only and then alternating one pick of weft rag in twill pattern with one pick of weft yarn in plain weave. Weave until 57¾ in (146 cm) long or to desired length, then finish with 1 in (2.5 cm) of weft yarn in plain weave. Secure with 1 in (2.5 cm) of waste yarn, and cut from loom.

Finishing

Finished dimensions: 24¾ in (63 cm) x 50¾ in (129 cm), excluding hem

Using a sewing machine, stitch straight across the beginning and end of desk runner right at the edge of the hem (between the waste yarn and the hem). Go back and zigzag stitch in the same area, being careful to get all the way to the selvedges. Using scissors, cut away waste yarn from beginning and end, being careful not to cut the sewing lines just made.

Follow wet-finishing instructions for **tencel warp/silk rag** on page 27. Machine-dry with a large towel on low or no heat, checking every 20 minutes, until dry. Using an iron set on low to medium, hard press with steam, using iron to square up corners and straighten ends.

Turn entire hem under rag-woven area and tack down on the back of the runner. Press the edge flat.

Care

Hand wash in cold water with mild detergent or shampoo. Rinse well and spin water out in washing machine set on spin. Dry and press as for **Finishing**.

Under the Sea Desk Runner

Threading

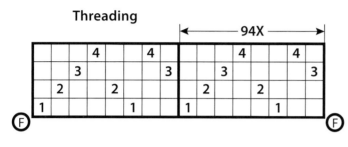

Tie-Up

X = Weft yarn
O = Weft rag
F = Floating selvedge

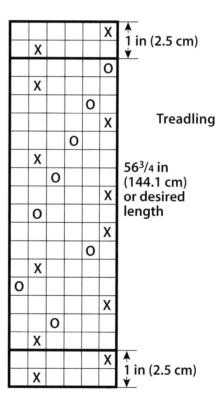

Treadling

1 in (2.5 cm)

56³/₄ in (144.1 cm) or desired length

1 in (2.5 cm)

Sundown Wall Hanging

When I saw this rayon dress (p. 94) in the thrift shop, I knew that whatever I made from it had to preserve the beautiful color gradient. I decided to make a wall hanging that is long and narrow, a common shape for Japanese wall décor.

The wall hanging is woven in plain weave with random bits of weft inlay to add visual interest and texture. I wanted the color areas to be distinct from each other, so I chose to stick with horizontal inlaid elements, but you could just as easily add supplementary warp pieces here and there for more vertical movement in the cloth.

In order for the warp not to show very much, I sett the ends farther apart than usual to get a mostly weft-faced weave.

Above: Additional yarns used for the weft inlay selections.

Above: A mostly weft-faced weave allows the color changes to shine.

Left: A striking color gradient is built right in to this dress.

Materials

Warp: 8/2 tencel (3,360 yd/lb), Valley Yarns, Straw, 318 yd (291 m)

Weft yarn: Small amount of warp yarn or other yarn matching the rags for fringe header and pocket hem; various yarns, rags, or other materials to use as weft inlay.

Weft rags: Rayon dress, cut into 1/2-in (1.3-cm) strips, preserving color order, approximately 105 yd (96 m)

Warping and Weaving

Sett: 10 EPI

Weave structure: Plain weave with weft inlay

Width in reed: 10 1/2 in (27 cm)

Wind a 3-yd (2.75-m) warp of 104 ends. Warp your loom by your desired method, setting the loom up for plain weave. Weave a header of at least an inch with waste yarn to spread the warp and provide an anchor for adding floating selvedges and a place to secure a temple.

After allowing at least 10 in (25 cm) of warp for fringe, under high tension, weave 1/2 in (1.3 cm) in plain weave with doubled warp yarn (or other weft yarn that matches the weft rags) only. Leave a tail of 32 in (81 cm) at the beginning and hemstitch in bundles of eight (nine at each selvedge edge to incorporate floating selvedge) and then switch to weft rag only. Place weft inlays where desired. Weave until 38 in (96.5 cm) long or to desired length, then finish with 1 1/2 in (3.8 cm) of doubled warp yarn (or other weft yarn that matches the weft rags) only. Secure with 1 in (2.5 cm) of waste yarn.

Sundown Wall Hanging

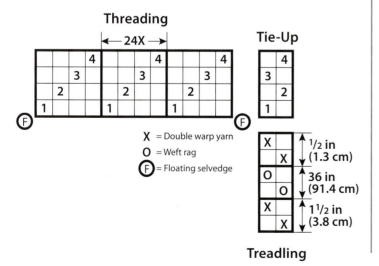

Finishing

Finished dimensions: 9 1/4 in (23.5 cm) x 35 in (89 cm), excluding rolled hem rod pocket and fringe

For the top edge (hem), using a sewing machine, zig-zag stitch across the beginning of the wall hanging right at the edge of the hem (between the waste yarn and the hem). Hand-sew the rolled hem into a pocket for inserting a hanging rod, as pictured below.

For the bottom edge (fringe), knot together in plain or lattice-style, or braid or twist, as desired, removing waste yarn.

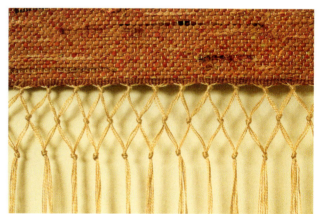

Care

Shake out to remove dust. When necessary, hand-wash in cold water with mild detergent, rinse well, and roll in a towel to press out excess water. Hang to dry and lightly press with a cool iron, if needed. If you are unsure of the colorfastness of any of the weft inlays that you used, the wall hanging should be dry cleaned instead of hand washed.

Rustic Wool Hearth Rug and Log Carrier

Wool is the ideal material for a hearth rug to protect your floors from sparks and embers from the fireplace, due to its natural fire resistance. For a thick and cushy hearth rug that is both unique and beautiful, look no further than the sweater racks of your local thrift shop. Felted wool strips make excellent rug weft!

Choose the colors you want, in sweaters that are 100% wool (sheep, alpaca, mohair, etc.) and are not labeled superwash or machine-washable. You will need six to ten adult sweaters, perhaps more if your hearth area is very large. Wash the sweaters, a few at a time, in hot water with detergent. Machine-dry, checking lint filter every 20 minutes to empty it. When they are dry, evaluate how felted they have become. If they still seem as if they may unravel when cut, repeat the washing and drying procedure.

When your sweaters are felted and ready to cut, get out your most comfortable heavy-duty shears. I like the kind that has very large handles and spring action to reduce hand fatigue. While you should definitely wear a dust mask while weaving these items, you may want one during cutting as well. I usually cover my lap with a large towel to catch the lint.

Starting at the waistband of each sweater, cut a 1-in (2.5-cm) strip in one long spiral up through the body of the sweater. When you reach the armholes, you may go back and forth across the chest as far as you can. Cut the sleeves in the same manner, and the remaining flat piece from the upper back can be cut in a continuous strip by cutting back and forth. Wind the felted sweater yarn into balls.

Don't worry about thick side seams or the corners where you cut back and forth. As you weave, keep a pair of scissors handy to trim down any of these areas that are too different in thickness to leave in. Remember, though, that the rug is meant to be rustic in style and the lumps and bumps add to its charm.

As long as we are making a hearth rug, why not make a matching log carrier as well? A simple log carrier is really nothing more than a rag rug with straps. Unless you are weaving a very narrow hearth rug, the log carrier will be narrower than the hearth rug. You could make two different warps for the two projects, but you also have the option of putting on one long warp, weaving and cutting off the hearth rug, and then cutting away enough warp threads from each selvedge to make the log carrier the correct width. Tie on and tension the center warp threads you are keeping, and weave the log carrier, ignoring the cut threads.

This hearth rug was made to fit a certain fireplace area, but you may have a different size you would like to make. It is important to know that when weaving with these heavy strips, your finished width will actually be wider than your warp threads in the reed by about 3–5 percent. Thus, the rug here, which was 30 in (76 cm) wide in the reed, is about 31½ in (80 cm) on the floor. There will also be more take-up of the warp, close to 20 percent. Be sure to take these factors into consideration when planning your project.

HEARTH RUG

Materials

Warp: 8/4 carpet warp (1,600 yd/lb), Maysville, Velvet, 2,187 yd (2,000 m)

Weft rags: Felted wool sweaters, cut into 1-in (2.5-cm) strips, 177 yd (162 m)

Warping and Weaving

Sett: 16 EPI (2 ends per dent in 8-dent reed)

Weave structure: Plain weave, but note that where wool strips are woven, two ends are raised or lowered as one unit, while in the hems each end moves independently (see chart)

Width in reed: 30 in (76 cm)

Wind a 4¾-yd (4.3-m) warp of 480 ends. Warp your loom by your desired method, following the chart given. Weave a plain weave header (as for hem) of at least an inch with waste yarn to spread the warp.

Under high tension, weave 1½-in (3.8-cm) hem in plain weave as indicated on the chart, using two strands of carpet warp wound together as one. Switch to rug body treadling and wool strips. Weave until 86½ in (220 cm) long or to desired length, then finish with another 1½ in (3.8 cm) hem. Secure with 1 in (2.5 cm) of waste yarn, and cut from loom.

Finishing

Finished dimensions: 31½ in (80 cm) x 72 in (183 cm) including hem

Using a sewing machine, zigzag stitch across the beginning and end of rug right at the edge of the hem (between the waste yarn and the hem). Using scissors, cut away waste yarn from beginning and end, being careful not to cut the sewing lines just made.

Hand-sew rolled hem on each end, taking care to be neat so that the rug can be reversible.

Care

Shake out or vacuum regularly. If needed, machine-wash in cold water with mild detergent or shampoo. Hang to dry. When completely dry, the rug may be tumbled in the dryer to remove excess lint, if desired.

LOG CARRIER

Materials

Warp: 8/4 carpet warp (1,600 yd/lb), Maysville, Velvet, 608 yd (556 m)

Weft rags: Felted wool sweaters, cut into 1-in (2.5-cm) strips, 58 yd (53 m)

Handles: 4 yd (3.6 m) of 1-in (2.5-cm) cotton webbing, matching strong sewing thread

Warping and Weaving

Sett: 16 EPI (2 ends per dent in 8-dent reed)

Weave structure: Plain weave, but note that where wool strips are woven, two ends are raised or lowered as one unit, while in the hems each end moves independently (see chart)

Width in reed: 18 in (45.75 cm)

Wind a 2¼-yd (2-m) warp of 288 ends. Warp your loom by your desired method, following the chart given. Weave a plain weave header (as for hem) of at least an inch (2.5 cm) with waste yarn to spread the warp.

Under high tension, weave a 1½-in (3.8-cm) hem in plain weave as indicated on the chart, using two strands of carpet warp wound together as one. Switch to rug body treadling and wool strips. Weave until 43 in (109.2 cm) long or to desired length, then finish with another 1½-in (3.8-cm) hem. Secure with 1 in (2.5 cm) of waste yarn, and cut from loom.

Finishing

Finished dimensions: 20 in (51 cm) x 38 in (96.5 cm),
including hem

Using a sewing machine, zigzag stitch across the beginning and end of carrier right at the edge of the hem (between the waste yarn and the hem).

Hand-sew rolled hem on each end. Sew straps to carrier as shown to form handles. (Unless you have a heavy-duty sewing machine, I recommend you take the carrier and your straps to a tailor for this step.)

Care

Shake out or vacuum regularly. If needed, machine-wash in cold water with mild detergent or shampoo. Hang to dry.

To Make Both the Rug and Carrier on the Same Warp

- Warp the loom as for the hearth rug, but wind a warp of 6 yd (5.4 m).
- Cut rug off slowly, 8 dents at a time, and tie the ends in slip knots to prevent them falling back behind the reed.
- Carefully untie and pull toward the back of the loom 96 ends (from 48 dents) on *each* selvedge edge of the warp, leaving 288 ends (36 dents) of center warp.
- Fix these warp ends to the cloth beam, tension warp, and then follow the weaving instructions for the Log Carrier.
- If you wish, you can save the longer pieces of waste warp created by this process to warp a small loom for mug rugs!

Rustic Wool Hearth Rug and Log Carrier

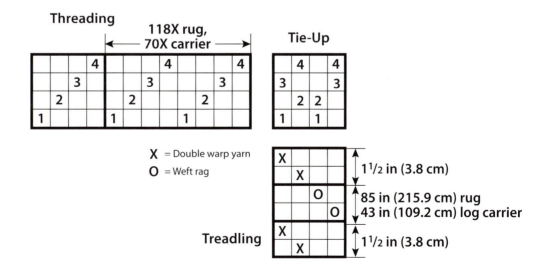

Weaving to Wear

S akiori was usually made into garments that were simple, uncut rectangles of woven material sewn together with minimal shaping. There are good reasons not to cut into handwoven material, especially if you are hoping to take your garment apart and make it into something else as needed. In today's world, we have an abundance of fabric and usually don't mind cutting it, but as handweavers we sometimes still have emotional barriers to cutting into the cloth we wove.

Because rag weaving produces an unbalanced material with a heavier weft, it has a tendency to fall apart when cut. This can be mitigated with stay-stitching and other techniques, but why not borrow from the Japanese tradition, and see what we can make without cutting up our cloth?

Flower Garden Overshot Shawl

A beautiful shawl is a great wardrobe piece—something you can use as a cover-up when it is a bit chilly or windy that complements, rather than detracts from, a dressy look. This piece would look great over a simple dress worn to an outdoor wedding.

A floral overshot border in contrasting rags provides a bit of elegant trim to the shawl ends.

Materials

Warp: 8/2 Rayon from bamboo (3,360 yd/lb), Halcyon Yarn, Magenta, 1,796 yd (1642 m), plus extra for weft in overshot areas

Weft yarn: 10/2 tencel (4,200 yd/lb), Just Our Yarn hand-dyed, Almaza, 825 yd (754 m); small amount of warp yarn

Weft rags: Silk garments, cut into ½-in (1.3-cm) strips

Warping and Weaving

Sett: 16 EPI

Weave structure: Overshot, Ring Around A Rosey, Design 62 from *Weaving Designs by Bertha Gray Hayes* (Figure 153) (*Weaving Designs by Bertha Gray Hayes: Miniature Overshot Patterns,* by Norma Smayda, Gretchen White, Jody Brown, and Katharine Schelleng, Atglen, PA: Schiffer, 2009).

Width in reed: 29.9 in (76 cm)

Wind a 3¾-yd (3.4 m) warp of 463 ends. Warp your loom by your desired method, following the chart given. After allowing at least 8 in (20 cm) of warp yarn for fringe, weave a header of at least an inch (2.5 cm) with waste yarn to spread the warp and provide an anchor for adding floating selvedges and a place to secure a temple. If desired, begin with leaving a 90-in (2.3-m) weft yarn tail for hemstitching.

Under high tension, weave in plain weave, beginning with six picks of weft yarn only and then alternating one pick of weft rag with two picks of weft yarn. Weave for 4 in (10 cm), cutting weft rag and weft yarn and weaving in ends. *Weave two picks of dark contrast rag with warp yarn as weft yarn. Switch to solid light weft rag and, continuing to use warp yarn as overshot area weft yarn, begin overshot pattern, weaving one pick weft rag in pattern alternating with one pick weft yarn in plain weave. Finish chart, cut pattern weft rag, and weave in ends. Resuming plain weave, weave one pick of dark contrast rag, two picks of warp yarn as weft yarn, and cut and weave in the end of the warp yarn used as weft yarn. Weave one more pick of dark contrast rag, then cut and weave in end.* Weave two picks of tencel weft

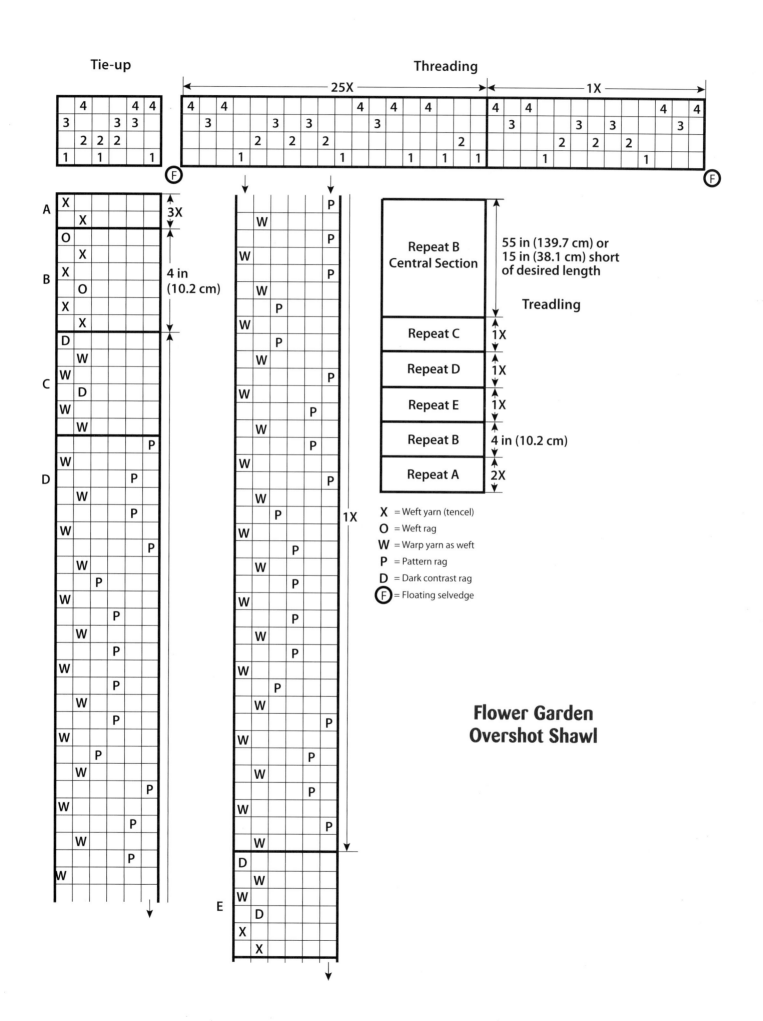

Tie-up

Threading

Flower Garden Overshot Shawl

55 in (139.7 cm) or
15 in (38.1 cm) short
of desired length

Treadling

Repeat B Central Section	
Repeat C	1X
Repeat D	1X
Repeat E	1X
Repeat B	4 in (10.2 cm)
Repeat A	2X

X = Weft yarn (tencel)
O = Weft rag
W = Warp yarn as weft
P = Pattern rag
D = Dark contrast rag
Ⓕ = Floating selvedge

yarn in plain weave. Resume plain weave pattern with weft rag and weft yarn. Weave to 8 in (20 cm) short of the desired length, ending with a weft yarn pick, cutting and weaving in weft rag and weft yarn ends. Repeat from * to *. Resume plain weave pattern for 4 in (10 cm), finishing with six picks of weft yarn, and hemstitching, if desired. Secure with 1 in (2.5 cm) of waste yarn, and cut from loom, allowing at least 8 in (20 cm) for fringe.

Finishing

Finished dimensions: 26½ in (67 cm) x 64½ in (164 cm), excluding fringe

Finish fringe as desired. Twisting or braiding is recommended to keep the fine yarns from tangling and fraying in washing and wearing the scarf.

Follow wet-finishing instructions for **bamboo warp/ silk rag** on page 27. Machine-dry with a large towel on low or no heat, checking every 20 minutes, until dry.

Using an iron set on low to medium, hard press with steam, using iron to square up corners and straighten ends.

Care

Hand-wash in cold water with mild detergent or shampoo. Rinse well and spin water out in washing machine set on spin. Dry and press as for **Finishing**.

I See Fire: Keyhole Scarf with Beads

*Watch the flames burn
auburn on
the mountain side
Desolation comes
upon the sky
Now I see fire
Inside the mountain
I see fire
Burning the trees*
—Ed Sheeran,
"I See Fire"

I am a confirmed Tolkien nerd, and I loved it when director Peter Jackson made *The Lord of the Rings* and *The Hobbit* into movies. Jackson was mindful in all his choices for the films, from the sweeping scenery in his native New Zealand used as the backdrop for Middle Earth to the rare Stansborough sheep chosen to provide the wool for many of the costumes. The music in the movies was excellent, but I especially loved the haunting ballad "I See Fire," written and performed by Ed Sheeran, which played during the end credits of *The Hobbit: The Desolation of Smaug* (2013).

Because silk takes dye so readily, it is often dyed into bright, vibrant colors. Although these colors are beautiful as accents, they can be overwhelming when an entire garment is made from them. The reds, oranges, and yellows of living flame that are in this scarf were rescued from garments that would be unlikely to flatter most wearers, but make a wonderful touch to a more sedate background.

As much jewelry as scarf, this bright bit of color with sparkling Swarovski crystal beads sits closely around the neck to enhance any outfit. A keyhole is woven into one end of the scarf so that both ends of the scarf, with their decorative beads and short twisted fringe, can be shown off.

Materials

Warp: 10/2 tencel (4,200 yd/lb), Just Our Yarn hand-dyed, Almaza, 189 yd (173 m)

Weft yarn: Same as warp yarn, 77 yd (70 m)

Weft rags: Lightweight silk from various garments, cut into ½-in (1.3-cm) strips (approximately 25 yd [23 m] of strips)

Beads: 30 Swarovski crystals, Crystal Passions, light smoked topaz, 6 mm Xilion bicones

Tools for making keyhole: Waste yarn or string, small weights (such as a couple of large washers), extra boat shuttle, and bobbins

AMANDA ROBINETTE

String and weights are used to make a keyhole guide.

I See Fire: Keyhole Scarf with Beads

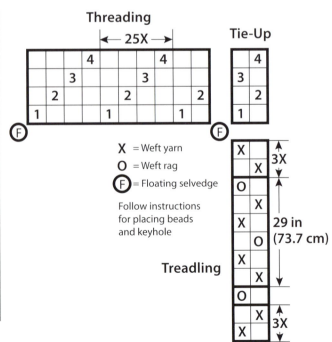

X = Weft yarn

O = Weft rag

F = Floating selvedge

Follow instructions for placing beads and keyhole

This scarf is too narrow for even the smallest of regular temples, so I chose to weave without one. If you don't want to go without, consider using a Leclerc Clip Temple or a homemade one. Weavers sometimes make these temples by putting a clip on the selvedge with a weighted cord that hangs over a rod secured parallel to the selvedge a few inches from the weaving. An internet search for "homemade temple for weaving" will provide you with some examples to work from.

Warping and Weaving

Sett: 20 EPI (2 ends per dent in a 10-dent reed)
Weave structure: Plain weave
Width in reed: 5¼ in (13 cm)

Wind a 1¾-yd (1.6-m) warp of 106 ends and warp your loom by your desired method. Set up the loom for plain weave. After allowing at least 4 in (10 cm) of warp yarn for fringe, weave a header of at least an inch (2.5 cm) with waste yarn to spread the warp and provide an anchor for adding floating selvedges.

If desired, begin with leaving a 16 in (41 cm) weft yarn tail for hemstitching. Under high tension, weave in plain weave, beginning with six picks of weft yarn only. Weave one pick of weft rag, followed by two picks of weft yarn. Cut weft yarn and weave in the end. Weave one more pick of weft rag.

Adding the Beads

Next, thread 15 beads onto the end of the weft yarn coming from your shuttle. (See photo tutorial on p. 114.) Hold the end of the thread tightly to keep the beads from sliding off. Begin by opening the next shed. Put the shuttle through six of the raised warp threads, then bring the shuttle and all the beads up through the shed. Take a moment to overlap and weave in the end of the weft yarn. *Keeping the shed open, slide three beads close to the weaving, then pass the shuttle with remaining beads over five of the raised warp threads and back into the shed. Pass it under four of the raised warp threads and bring it back to the top with all remaining beads. Adjust the weft yarn so that the three beads are not tight against the cloth to prevent puckering of the fabric. The beads should lie in a loose arc across the fabric, like a necklace.

Repeat from * until all beads have been placed. Pass the shuttle under the last six raised warp threads and out of the shed. Make a final check on the weft yarn tension and beat. If the draw-in from beating made any of the beads too tight, adjust the weft yarn and beat again.

Forming the Keyhole

Weave in pattern as established (one pick weft rag alternating with two picks of weft yarn) until piece measures 3 in (7.6 cm) from beginning, not including fringe allowance, ending after a weft yarn pick. Find the center of the warp threads (54 ends on each side, including floating selvedges). Cut a piece of waste yarn or string about 20 in (51 cm) long and tie it to the washers. Tie the other end to the top beater bar and drop the length of yarn with the washers at the bottom through the warp threads at the halfway point. The yarn should be long enough for the beater to move forward without pulling

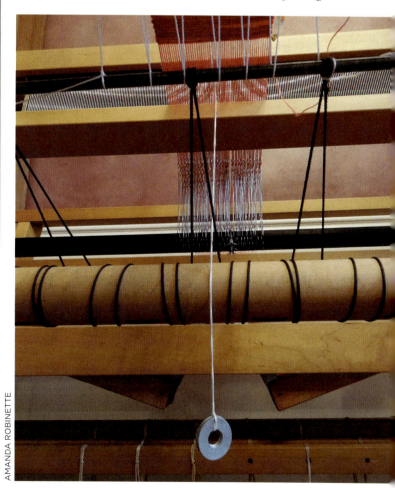

AMANDA ROBINETTE

The keyhole guide in place, as viewed from underneath the front of the loom.

Adding Beads

1 To place the beads, first string the desired number of beads on the weft thread and secure the end of weft thread in the weaving. Open the next shed and pass the shuttle, with all beads, through the first group of warp threads, then bring the shuttle and beads up and out of the shed.

2 Slide the desired number of beads into place across the next group of warp threads, then pass the shuttle with all remaining beads back into the shed through the third group of warp threads and out of the shed again.

3 Adjust the weft yarn to allow for draw-in so that the first group of beads is not pulled too tightly against the fabric. They should rest on the fabric like a necklace, but without a lot of extra weft yarn showing. Slide the next group of beads into place.

4 You can determine how loosely the beads will lie on the fabric by gently pulling the beater forward until draw-in of the weft yarn occurs. It is easier to make adjustments as you go than to wait until all beads have been placed.

5 Repeat this process until all beads have been placed and the weft yarn has been adjusted across the width of the warp. Beat, change sheds, and beat again to secure weft yarn in place.

The keyhole forms in the cloth. Note the string of the keyhole guide between the warp threads near the beater.

The finished keyhole, as viewed from underneath the loom.

the washers up through the shed, but not so long that it will become tangled in the loom or your legs.

Using the weighted string as a guide, begin weaving each side independently in pattern, using the extra boat shuttle and passing the shuttles in the same direction on each pick. A slit will form in the cloth as you proceed. When the slit measures 2¾ in (7 cm) or just short of that, cut and weave in the weft yarn on one half. Weave one more pick of weft rag, then cut and weave the end in on the same half. You should now have one shuttle with weft yarn and one rag strip together on the same selvedge.

Now, remove the weighted string from the loom and resume weaving the full width of the warp, beginning with a weft yarn pick.

Adding the Second Row of Beads

Weave until piece measures around 28 in (71 cm), not including fringe allowance, or about an inch (2.5 cm) shorter than desired weaving length. Following instructions above, place another row of beads.

Continue weaving in pattern until two weft rag picks have been placed after the beads, ending after the second weft rag pick. Finish with six picks of weft yarn, and hemstitching, if desired. Secure with 1 in (2.5 cm) of waste yarn, and cut from loom, allowing at least 4 in (10 cm) for fringe.

Finishing

Finished dimensions: 4½ in (11 cm) x 27 in (68.5 cm), excluding fringe

Finish fringe as desired. Twisting or braiding is recommended to keep the fine yarns from tangling and fraying in washing and wearing the scarf.

Follow wet-finishing instructions for **tencel warp/silk rag** on page 27. Hang to dry. If desired, roll scarf up in a towel, place in a pillowcase, and secure tightly by tying, and place in dryer on low heat for 20 minutes to soften scarf without damaging the beads. Using an iron set on low to medium, hard press with steam, using iron to square up corners and straighten ends.

Care

Hand wash in cold water with mild detergent or shampoo. Rinse well and spin water out in a salad spinner or roll in towel and press to remove excess water. Dry and press as for **Finishing**.

Men's Vintage Bowling Shirt

One easy way to use sakiori to make clothing is to insert panels wherever a rectangular shape already exists. This can be done by modifying garments (re-fashioning) or by making a new garment and using sakiori as pattern pieces. If you are a confident sewer and like to make your own patterns, the sky's the limit. But there are some choices for those who prefer to have a set of instructions to follow, as well!

By flipping through books of sewing patterns, you will be able to find patterns for clothes that have at least one rectangular (or almost-rectangular) element. Think about the placement of that piece in the finished item and about whether it would be a good place for a decorative element. Then, simply substitute a piece of sakiori that you have woven to the desired measurements for the pattern piece you wish to replace.

To illustrate this, I have chosen a men's vintage bowling shirt, with two convenient rectangular contrast stripes, one on each side of the shirt front. The stripes have only a slight curve to bend out toward the shoulder. I had several options for dealing with this curve. One of the shirt options has a pocket that falls directly over the start of the curve, and I could have cut the sakiori panel and used a shaped piece of the shirt fabric to re-orient the direction of the panel when it emerges from the top of the pocket. Alternatively, another type of decorative element could have been placed over the area where shaping was needed.

In the end, the simplest solution prevailed, and darts were used to turn the panels. Once pressed down, there is no additional bulk and only someone trying to figure out the construction would notice the dart's seam.

Modifying garments and patterns is your chance to let your own creativity shine.

Materials

Warp: 8/2 tencel (3,360 yd/lb), Valley Yarns, Black, 237 yd (217 m)

Weft yarn: Same as warp yarn, 120 yd (110 m)

Weft rags: Lightweight silk from several garments, cut into ½-in (1.3-cm) strips (approximately 60 yd [55 m] of strips)

Sewing materials: McCall's Pattern M7206, Men's Shirts; Fabric/Notions as listed for pattern option B; 1-in (2.5-cm) wide single-fold bias tape to match sakiori panel

Warping and Weaving

Sett: 16 EPI (2 ends per dent in an 8-dent reed)

Weave structure: Plain weave

Width in reed: 5.4 in (14 cm)

Wind a 2¾-yd (2.5-m) warp of 86 ends and warp your loom by your desired method. Set up the loom for plain weave. Weave a header of at least an inch with waste yarn to spread the warp and provide an anchor for adding floating selvedges.

AMANDA ROBINETTE

Under high tension, weave in plain weave, beginning with 1 in (2.5 cm) of weft yarn only and then alternating one pick of weft rag with two picks of weft yarn. Weave for 67½ in (171.5 cm) or to the desired length, then finish with 1 in (2.5 cm) of weft yarn only. Secure with 1 in (2.5 cm) of waste yarn, and cut from loom.

Finishing

Finished dimensions: 4⅝ in (12 cm) x 62 in (157 cm)

Using a sewing machine, stitch straight across the beginning and end of strip right at the edge of the hem (between the waste yarn and the hem). Go back and zigzag stitch in the same area, being careful to get all the way to the selvedges.

Using scissors, cut away waste yarn, being careful not to cut the sewing lines just made.

Follow wet-finishing instructions for **tencel warp/silk rag** on page 27. Machine-dry with a large towel on low or no heat, checking every 20 minutes, until dry. Using an iron set on low to medium, hard press with steam, using iron to square up corners and straighten ends.

I used cotton batik for the shirt. Whatever fabric you choose, be sure to wash and dry it before cutting and sewing. If it shrinks after sewing, the long seams between the sakiori panels and the shirt fabric will pucker.

Follow instructions for McCall's Pattern M7206 Option B in desired size. Make the following adjustments to the pattern:

* Additional notions: 1-in (2.5-cm) wide single-fold bias seam tape to match sakiori panel.
* The sakiori panels are used in place of pattern piece #2 (Contrast, Middle Front).
* The plain weave hems on the sakiori panels correspond to the bottom edges of pieces #1 and #3, below.

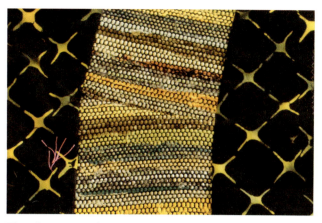

The dart turns the panel to correspond to the pattern piece.

* Determine the length needed for sakiori panels. Before cutting the panels, stitch straight across adjacent to and inside of the cutting line. Go back and zigzag along the same line, then cut along cutting line.
* To adjust the sakiori panels to the curve of the front and side edges of pattern piece #2, place a ⅝-in (1.5-cm) dart on sakiori panels at side edge (piece #3) single notch that extends to within 1 in (2.5 cm) of the front edge of sakiori panel. Press dart seam down towards hem edge of sakiori panel.

* For pattern steps 2 and 3, sew the front, middle front (sakiori panel), and side front as instructed.
* Do not press seams towards middle front (sakiori panel); instead, press front edge seam towards front edge and side front seam towards side front. These steps minimize adding bulk to the seams under the sakiori panel.
* Encase cut edge of sakiori panels in 1-in (2.5-cm) wide single-fold bias seam tape.
* For pattern step 18, top stitch side front instead of middle front (sakiori panel).
* For pattern step 20, top stitch front instead of middle front (sakiori panel).
  Finish shirt as instructed in pattern.

Care

This shirt should be dry-cleaned for best results, due to the long seams between different types of fabric that may cause puckering when washed.

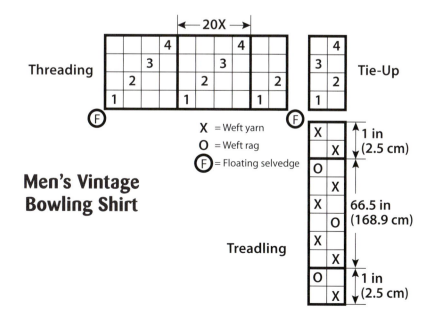

Men's Vintage Bowling Shirt

Threading

Tie-Up

Treadling

X = Weft yarn
O = Weft rag
F = Floating selvedge

20X

1 in (2.5 cm)

66.5 in (168.9 cm)

1 in (2.5 cm)

Elegant Evening Bag with Silk and Leather

Although leather cannot properly be termed a textile, I think it ought to be included in any discussion of textile waste. It is a material from which clothing, household goods, and other necessaries such as shoes and purses are made, and can be used interchangeably with textiles for these purposes.

Just like textiles, there is a flood of leather items being thrown away or taken to thrift shops. Leather made into garments or upholstery is pliable enough to cut into strips for rag weaving. Only space considerations are holding me back from attempting a leather rag rug made from someone's discarded leather sofa!

In a nod to such considerations, I instead offer this small evening handbag made from a black leather skirt and some red-and-black silk from a ladies' dress. The resulting sakiori has a substantial, but soft and pliable, hand. The bag itself is a simple rectangle forming a foldover bag, lined with silk rag and using a chain strap with a clever screwback attachment.

Materials

Warp: Bambu 7 (2,100 yd/lb), Silk City Fibers, Onyx 360, 135 yd (123 m)

Weft yarn: Same as warp

Weft rags: Leather from skirt, cut into ¼-in (.6-cm) strips; and lightweight silk from ladies' dress, cut into ½-in (1.3-cm) strips (approximately 32 yd [29 m] of strips)

The thin leather of the skirt, with lining and seams removed.

A clear cutting guide and rotary cutter can easily make very thin strips for weaving.

Bag Construction Materials

Lining: 7½ in (19 cm) x 22 in (56 cm) satin or brocade, plus a piece 4½ in (11 cm) x 3½ in (9 cm) for pocket (if desired), 7½ in (19 cm) x 22 in (56 cm) interfacing (if desired); sewing thread to match handwoven and lining fabric; purse findings (40 in [102 cm] strap

and D-rings or screwback button studs with D-rings, as desired); strong sewing thread for D-rings (if not using screwback type)

Warping and Weaving

Sett: 12 EPI

Weave structure: Plain weave

Width in reed: 7½ in (19 cm)

Wind a 1½-yd (1.3-m) warp of 90 ends and warp your loom by your desired method. Set up the loom for plain weave. Weave a header of at least an inch with waste yarn to spread the warp and provide an anchor for adding floating selvedges and a place to secure a temple.

Under high tension, weave in plain weave, beginning with ½ in (1.3 cm) of warp yarn only and then alternating one pick of leather with two picks of silk rag. Weave for 24½ in (62 cm) or to the desired length, finishing with ½ in (1.3 cm) of warp yarn hem. Secure with 1 in (2.5 cm) of waste yarn, and cut from loom.

Finishing

Finished dimensions: 7½ in (19 cm) x 22 in (56 cm)

Cut one piece of lining fabric 7½ x 22 in (19 x 56 cm) or the same size as the body. Using a sewing machine, zigzag the narrow ends (which will be at the top of the bag) to tidy them. Fold the bag fabric with right sides together, matching the side (long) edges and top (short) edges and lining up the stripe design to match. Pin edges. Machine-stitch the sides only, leaving the top open. Repeat these sewing instructions for the lining, leaving a 4–5" opening on one long side. Turn the lining right side out. Slip the

lining inside the bag, with right sides facing and matching top edges. Topstitch the lining to the bag along the top edges. Reach your hand into the bag and through the opening in the lining. Turn the bag right side out by pulling it through the opening in the lining. Fold the seam allowances in the opening of the lining and pin in place. Sew the opening closed. Attach the purse findings.

Care

Spot clean as needed. If necessary, take to a professional dry cleaner.

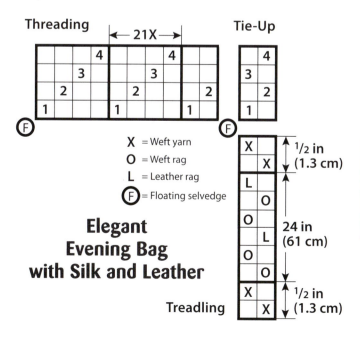

Threading

← 21X →

			4				4		
		3				3			
	2				2				2
1				1				1	

Ⓕ

Tie-Up

	4
3	
	2
1	

Ⓕ

X = Weft yarn
O = Weft rag
L = Leather rag
Ⓕ = Floating selvedge

Elegant Evening Bag with Silk and Leather

Treadling

X	
	X
L	
	O
O	
	L
O	
	O
X	
	X

½ in (1.3 cm)

24 in (61 cm)

½ in (1.3 cm)

The screwback attachment makes it easy to attach this strap to the bag.

A Necktie for the Modern Gentleman

Neckties, as we know them today, have only been around for 100 years or so. (Before their current iteration, there were cravats, ascots, and other versions of neckwear.) They are about as non-functional as a wardrobe piece can get, existing solely for decoration. Over time, ties have been wide, narrow, long, short, painted, plain, pointed, flat-bottomed, novelty-themed, knitted, woven, silk, polyester . . .

At times, men's fashion attempts to rid itself of ties (think Tom Cruise's character in 1988's *Rain Man*), make ties more casual (loose tie, open collar), and even camouflage tie-wearing by making sure the color of the necktie exactly matches that of the shirt.

In today's casual work culture, neckties are rarely worn. Like all things "fashion," the tide will probably turn one day and maybe future generations will sport the wide, short ties of the 1960s and 1970s.

In the meantime, the modern gentleman needs something fashionable to wear around his neck. This scarf, rising from the ashes of neckties past, fits the bill perfectly.

Materials

Warp: Laceweight tencel (2,520 yd/lb), Prism Delicato Layers, Slate, 330 yd (302 m)

Weft yarn: Same as warp yarn, 115 yd (106 m)

Weft rags: Silk from seven neckties, cut into ½-in (1.3-cm) strips (approximately 60 yd [55 m] of strips)

Warping and Weaving

Sett: 12 EPI

Weave structure: Plain weave

Width in reed: 9 in (23 cm)

Wind a 3-yd (2.75-m) warp of 108 ends and warp your loom by your desired method. Set up the loom for plain weave. After allowing at least 8 in (20 cm) of warp yarn for fringe, weave a header of at least an inch (2.5 cm) with waste yarn to spread the warp and provide an anchor for adding floating selvedges and a place to secure a temple. If desired, begin with leaving a 27-in (68.5-cm) weft yarn tail for hemstitching.

Under high tension, weave in plain weave, beginning with six picks of weft yarn only and then alternating one pick of weft rag with two picks of weft yarn. Weave

I made this scarf on a rigid heddle loom without using a temple, to illustrate the success that can be achieved with this simple, inexpensive loom by using the modifications described in **Rag Weaving on a Rigid Heddle Loom** (p. 25).

for 70 in (178 cm) or to the desired length, finishing with six picks of weft yarn, and hemstitching, if desired. Secure with 1 in (2.5 cm) of waste yarn, and cut from loom, allowing at least 8 in (20 cm) for fringe.

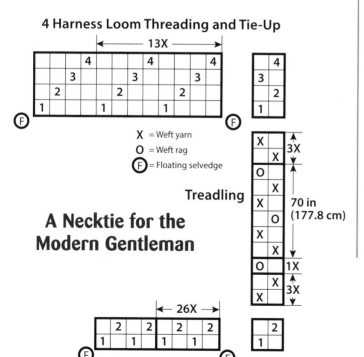

4 Harness Loom Threading and Tie-Up

13X

X = Weft yarn
O = Weft rag
F = Floating selvedge

Treadling

70 in (177.8 cm)

3X
1X
3X

A Necktie for the Modern Gentleman

26X

2 Harness Loom Threading and Tie-Up

Finishing

Finished dimensions: 6 in (15.25 cm) x 70 in (178 cm) excluding fringe

Finish fringe as desired. Twisting or braiding is recommended to keep the fine yarns from tangling and fraying in washing and wearing the scarf.

Follow wet-finishing instructions for **tencel warp/silk rag** on page 27. Machine-dry with a large towel on low or no heat, checking every 20 minutes, until dry. Using an iron set on low to medium, hard press with steam, using iron to square up corners and straighten ends.

Care

Hand-wash in cold water with mild detergent or shampoo. Rinse well and spin water out in washing machine set on spin or in a salad spinner. Dry and press as for **Finishing**.

TIFFANY BLACKSTONE PHOTOGRAPHY

Sodenashi

Sodenashi, Japanese, sleeveless garment

A sakiori sodenashi was a common utilitarian garment in rural Japan. Rugged enough for hard work, it could be worn alone or over other shirts. Sleeves made from larger cotton scraps could be added to protect arms from the hot sun in the summer or from the cold in the winter, and they can be easily removed or replaced as desired. Foresters, fishermen, and farmers all wore sodenashi.

Once I had learned how to weave my version of sakiori with materials like silk, tencel, and bamboo, I knew that I wanted to try my hand at a modern version of a work sodenashi. I wanted to undertake this traditional garment so that I could have a deeper appreciation of the history of sakiori and the lives of the women who made it, and also to show that this old form of garment can be relevant today.

COURTESY OF SRI, BROOKLYN, NY: AMANDA ROBINETTE

Note that I used the same elongated twill that I have used in other projects, but the traditional weave structure would be plain weave, as in the Basic Western Sakiori Scarf (p. 32). If you want a very traditional garment, use cotton rag on a hemp warp and make yours in plain weave.

In actual antique sodenashi, seams were sewn in many different ways. Some were purposefully visible, some were coarse, and some were carefully done with small stitches. Sodenashi are homemade garments and each one is made to the preference of the maker, whether they are following a village custom, the teaching of a mother, or something they came up with on their own. So relax—there is no wrong way to sew your sodenashi!

Detail of back seam on an antique sodenashi.

Other than a little machine zigzagging before the wet-finishing process and in creating the collar notches, I made my sodenashi entirely by hand. I followed in the footsteps of weavers before me as I washed the rags, cut them into strips, warped my loom and wove the two long rectangles. (I did not grow my own hemp and spin it into warp yarn, nor did I climb a mountain to find wisteria and linden for bast warp, for which I am grateful.) I cut up and dyed silk rag to make my own bias tape for the edging, and overdyed silk rag for the collar. I then hand-stitched the entire piece with silk thread. Last, I made a *kumihimo* braid for the front middle edge trim (this part is extremely non-traditional, since kumihimo was something for the wealthy and sakiori clothing was for the poor).

I am not going to give instructions to make the exact same sodenashi that I made, but rather a basic sodenashi, to which you can make your own unconventional additions and subtractions. Like everything else in this book, it is intended to spark ideas and get you thinking about ways to use your sakiori, not to be a pattern that you follow to a T.

More details about this garment can be found on my blog, at www.westernsakiori.com.

Materials

Warp: 8/2 tencel (3,360 yd/lb), Valley Yarns, Navy, 782 yd (715 m)

Weft yarn: Same as warp yarn, 304 yd (278 m)

Weft rags: Lightweight silk from many garments, cut into $\frac{1}{2}$-in (1.3-cm) strips (approximately 152 yd [139 m] of strips)

Sewing materials: Sewing thread, lightweight interfacing (if desired), bias tape or seam binding (if desired), extra material for collar, tailor's chalk or fabric marking pen

Warping and Weaving

Sett: 24 EPI

Weave structure: Twill, see chart

Width in reed: 7.87 in (20 cm)

Wind a $4\frac{1}{4}$-yd (3.8-m) warp of 184 ends and warp your loom by your desired method, following chart for twill pattern. Weave a header of at least an inch with waste yarn to spread the warp and provide an anchor for adding floating selvedges and a place to secure a temple.

*Under high tension, weave 1 in (2.5 cm) in plain weave of weft yarn only. Then alternate weaving one pick of weft rag in pattern with one pick of weft yarn in plain weave. Weave for 59 in (150 cm) or to the desired length, finishing with 1 in (2.5 cm) hem of weft yarn. Weave a few picks of waste yarn and repeat from * for

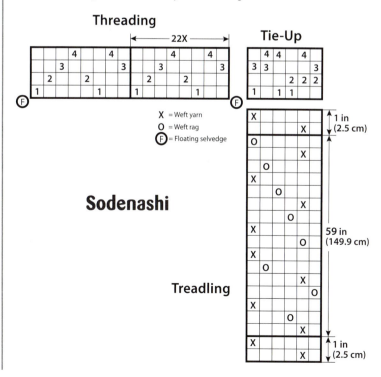

Threading

Tie-Up

X = Weft yarn
O = Weft rag
F = Floating selvedge

Sodenashi

Treadling

second sodenashi panel. Finish the second panel by weaving at least 1 in (2.5 cm) of waste yarn to secure ends, and cut from loom.

Finishing

Finished dimensions: 7.1 in (17.75 cm) x 51.2 in (130 cm) for each panel

Using a sewing machine, stitch straight across the beginning and end of the entire strip of two panels right at the edge of the hem (between the waste yarn and the hems). Go back and zigzag stitch in the same area, being careful to get all the way to the selvedges. Using scissors, cut away waste yarn from beginning and end, being careful not to cut the sewing lines just made.

On either side of the waste yarn between the two panels, repeat the straight stitching and zig-zag stitching, but do not cut panels apart yet.

Follow wet-finishing instructions for **tencel warp/silk rag** on page 27. Machine-dry with a large towel on low or no heat, checking every 20 minutes, until dry. Using an iron set on low to medium, hard press with steam, using iron to square up corners and straighten ends.

Using scissors, cut away waste yarn from the middle to separate the two panels, being careful not to cut the sewing lines.

Assembly of Sodenashi

Lay the two pieces side by side. Measure to find the halfway point of each piece and mark on the center edge. Draw a rectangle with fabric marking pen from .2 in (.5 cm) in front of the center mark to 1 in (2.5 cm) behind it, and 2 in (5 cm) in from the center edge. Straight-stitch twice just outside of the rectangles, and

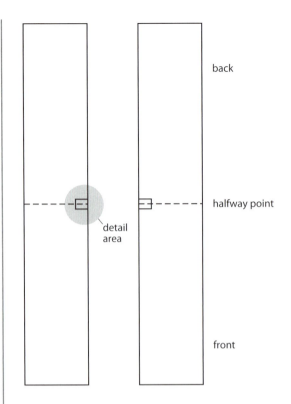

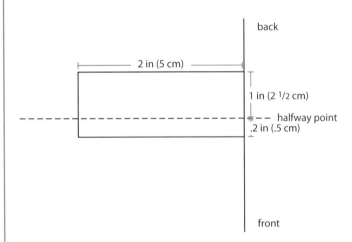

Detail of back seam.

On this muslin, the front pieces have been pressed back and tacked down with a few stitches.

You may notice that the rectangular collar facing does not want to lie neatly around the curve of the back of the neck. In that area, rather than binding the edge snugly with the collar facing, sew the facing edges to the edge of the vest so that the collar stands above the vest and the facing bunches up and creases to make the turns. Arrange it the way you want it before you sew it down! If desired, you can tack down the top edge of the center back collar facing so it is not as tall behind the neck.

The extra collar fabric has been tacked down for a neater appearance.

Bias tape and decorative kumihimo have been applied to all edges except where collar facing will cover.

The vest front and back edges are connected by strips of bias tape.

with sharp scissors carefully cut out the rectangles along the marked lines. If desired, apply Fray Check to cut edges. Next, pin together the back seam and hand-sew the seam from the neck edge (where you cut the rectangles out) to the hems.

Try on the vest (it is still open on the sides) and enlarge cutout area at neck, if desired, so that vest hangs well. Fold down the point of each center neck edge and tack it down with a few stitches. Press firmly. This will later be covered by the collar facing.

Sew rolled hems at all hem edges. Apply seam binding, bias tape, or preferred covering to both outside selvedge edges, all hems, and about halfway up the front center selvedges (or to the desired length of the collar).

Measure collar area from one center edge, around the neck, and to the other center edge. Cut a piece of fabric 4-in (10-cm) wide and that length plus ½ in (1.3 cm) for turning under at the front center to make a neat edge. Apply interfacing to the collar material, if desired. Sew collar facing around neck edge from center front. Cut away excess length from collar facing after reaching the center front of the other side.

Connect vest sides by sewing a band or two strips between each front and the back.

Care

You should have your sodenashi dry-cleaned due to its construction.

Ideas and Inspiration

This student used cotton batik fabric from Malaysia and a tencel warp to make this shawl with an elemental color scheme.

Right: Another student, Mitchell Anderson, made this beautiful skirt from sakiori panels for her daughter, Christian. Mitchell writes, "The sakiori panels that I wove in Amanda's class were so beautiful that I wanted to create something unique. This untraditional design was inspired by a kilt that my son wore occasionally. I added black silk gussets to shape the skirt."

MITCHELL ANDERSON

Left and above: A sakiori table runner made by a student. The warp and weft yarn are tencel, and the rag is Malaysian batik cut in ¼-in (.6-cm) strips.

SUPPLIERS

These are the main suppliers of materials used in this book, but there are many other fabulous retailers out there. If you are having trouble finding what you need locally, give these suppliers a try.

Yarn and Weaving Equipment

WEBS (Valley Yarns)

75 Service Center Rd
Northampton, MA 01060
800-FOR-WEBS; www.yarn.com

Just Our Yarn

www.justouryarn.com

Yarn Barn of Kansas

930 Massachusetts Street
Lawrence, KS 66044
800-468-0035, www.yarnbarn-ks.com

Halcyon Yarn

12 School St
Bath, ME 04530
800-341-0282, www.halcyonyarn.com

Fabric

Sew What Fabrics

460 East Main Street
Wytheville, VA 24382
800-228-4573, www.batiks.com

Rag Cutter

Harry M. Fraser, Co. (Fraser Rag Cutter)
498 Trot Valley Rd.
Stuart, VA 24171
276-694-5824, www.fraserrug.com

ACKNOWLEDGMENTS

I have relied heavily on the exhibit catalog *Riches from Rags: Saki-Ori & Other Recycling Traditions in Japanese Rural Clothing* (Shin-Ichiro Yoshida and Dai Williams, San Francisco Craft & Folk Art Museum, 1994), regretfully out of print and difficult to come by. While there are other sources that mention sakiori, none has gathered as much information together in one place, in English.

I also wish to thank Stephen Szczepanek of Sri Gallery (Brooklyn, NY) for sharing his extensive knowledge and allowing me access to his collection of antique rural Japanese textiles for research and study. Seeing and handling these garments and other textiles has allowed me a much deeper understanding of sakiori than I would otherwise have had.

I would not have made this book, indeed, I would not be a weaver, if not for my Aunt Luann, to whom I am eternally grateful. She is the reason I took my first weaving class, and she gave me my first loom to get me started. Aunt Luann, you are a part of everything I weave and everything I write about weaving.

Special thanks must also be given to my teacher and mentor, Tom Knisely, who taught me beginning weaving many years ago. When I first shared my sakiori weaving and research with Tom, he offered me the interest, encouragement, and support I needed to take my work to the next level. Also, my thanks go to Roderick Owen, my braiding teacher, who has taught me so much and helped me to share my work with others.

This book would not be complete without the beautiful photographs of Kathy Eckhaus. A weaver and rug-hooker herself, she has a deep understanding of what weavers want to see in a textile photograph. Her support and encouragement have been as important as her photographs! Thanks, Kathy.

And, last but not least, I want to thank my family: my husband, Chris, who always believed I could do it; my children, Sabrina and Colin, who put up with a lot of absences during the making of this book; my parents, Mary Ellen and John Lenz, who supported me in every way they could, from providing office space to sewing (thanks, Mom!); and my parents-in-law, Kim and Billie Kaye Robinette, who drove hundreds of miles to deliver my first "big" loom many years ago.